THE
BLACK PANTHER
PARTY

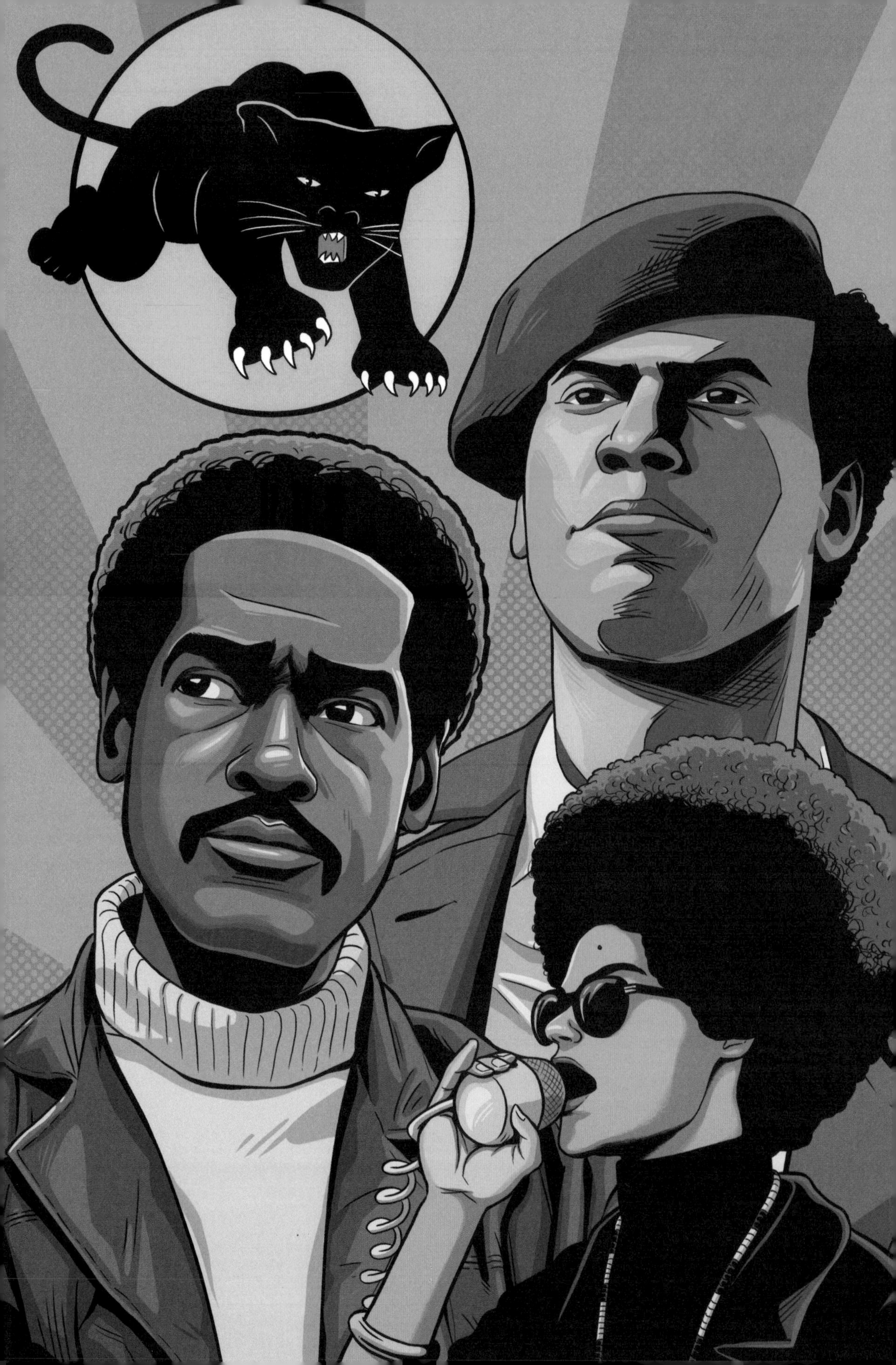

THE BLACK PANTHER PARTY

A GRAPHIC NOVEL HISTORY

DAVID F. WALKER

ART, COLORS, AND LETTERS BY
MARCUS KWAME ANDERSON

TEN SPEED PRESS
California | New York

"WE'VE GOT TO FACE THE FACT THAT SOME PEOPLE SAY YOU FIGHT FIRE BEST WITH FIRE, BUT WE SAY YOU PUT FIRE OUT BEST WITH WATER.

WE SAY YOU DON'T FIGHT RACISM WITH RACISM.

WE'RE GONNA FIGHT RACISM WITH SOLIDARITY."

—FRED HAMPTON

TO THE RANK AND FILE OF THE BLACK PANTHER PARTY—
THE BROTHERS AND SISTERS WHO COOKED MEALS
FOR THE FREE BREAKFAST FOR CHILDREN PROGRAM,
DELIVERED NEWSPAPERS, AND WHO LIVED AND DIED
FOR THE PEOPLE. YOU WERE THE HEART AND SOUL
OF THE PARTY, AND THIS BOOK IS FOR YOU.

CONTENTS

ONCE UPON A TIME, THERE WAS A GROUP KNOWN AS THE BLACK PANTHER PARTY FOR SELF-DEFENSE. FORMED IN OAKLAND, CA, BY HUEY P. NEWTON AND BOBBY SEALE IN 1966, THE PANTHERS DEFIANTLY STOOD IN STARK CONTRAST TO THE NONVIOLENT PHILOSOPHY OF THE MAINSTREAM CIVIL RIGHTS MOVEMENT.

THE BLACK PANTHERS TOOK UP ARMS, MARCHED IN THE STREETS, AND TOOK A CONFRONTATIONAL STAND AGAINST POLICE BRUTALITY. THEY CAPTURED THE ATTENTION OF THE NEIGHBORHOODS THEY PATROLLED, AND EVENTUALLY OF THE WORLD.

SOME PEOPLE ADMIRED THEM. SOME HATED THEM. IN TIME, THE BLACK PANTHERS BECAME MYTHICAL--AND IT CAN BE DIFFICULT TO SEPARATE MYTH FROM REALITY.

THE HISTORY OF THE BLACK PANTHER PARTY IS ONE LACED WITH VIOLENCE--IT IS ONE OF THE MOST ENDURING PARTS OF THE MYTH OF THE PANTHERS.

BUT VIOLENCE IS ONLY PART OF THE PANTHERS' STORY.

THE BLACK PANTHER PARTY WAS AN ORGANIZATION DEDICATED TO SERVING THE COMMUNITY.

THE PANTHERS CREATED MORE THAN 60 "SURVIVAL PROGRAMS" TO HELP COMMUNITIES ALL OVER THE COUNTRY, INCLUDING THE FREE BREAKFAST FOR SCHOOL CHILDREN PROGRAM, WHICH FED THOUSANDS OF CHILDREN EVERY WEEK.

PEOPLE'S FREE FOOD

THE BLACK PANTHER PARTY WAS A COMPLEX ORGANIZATION THAT HAD AN EQUALLY COMPLEX RELATIONSHIP WITH THE COMMUNITIES IT WAS DEDICATED TO SERVING.

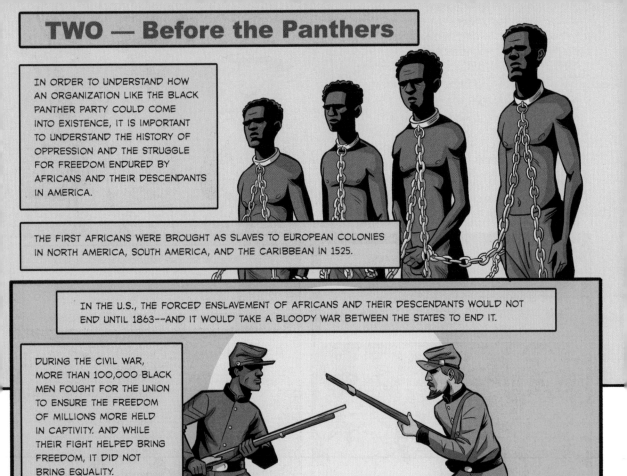

IN ORDER TO UNDERSTAND HOW AN ORGANIZATION LIKE THE BLACK PANTHER PARTY COULD COME INTO EXISTENCE, IT IS IMPORTANT TO UNDERSTAND THE HISTORY OF OPPRESSION AND THE STRUGGLE FOR FREEDOM ENDURED BY AFRICANS AND THEIR DESCENDANTS IN AMERICA.

THE FIRST AFRICANS WERE BROUGHT AS SLAVES TO EUROPEAN COLONIES IN NORTH AMERICA, SOUTH AMERICA, AND THE CARIBBEAN IN 1525.

IN THE U.S., THE FORCED ENSLAVEMENT OF AFRICANS AND THEIR DESCENDANTS WOULD NOT END UNTIL 1863--AND IT WOULD TAKE A BLOODY WAR BETWEEN THE STATES TO END IT.

DURING THE CIVIL WAR, MORE THAN 100,000 BLACK MEN FOUGHT FOR THE UNION TO ENSURE THE FREEDOM OF MILLIONS MORE HELD IN CAPTIVITY. AND WHILE THEIR FIGHT HELPED BRING FREEDOM, IT DID NOT BRING EQUALITY.

THE LEGACY OF RACIAL OPPRESSION THAT ALLOWED SLAVERY TO FLOURISH IN AMERICA FOR CENTURIES CONTINUED, AS BLACK AMERICANS STRUGGLED AGAINST DISCRIMINATION AND SEGREGATION, LOOKING TO FIND THEIR PLACE IN THE LAND OF THE FREE.

HAVING BEEN SUBJECTED TO CENTURIES OF DEHUMANIZING ATROCITIES LARGELY IN THE SOUTHERN STATES, MANY BLACK AMERICANS BEGAN TO MIGRATE TO THE NORTH AND WEST STARTING IN 1916.

KNOWN AS THE GREAT MIGRATION, BLACK AMERICANS FLED THE SOUTH BY THE MILLIONS LOOKING FOR A BETTER WAY OF LIFE, AWAY FROM LEGALIZED SEGREGATION, SHARECROPPING, AND LYNCHING.

LIFE OUTSIDE OF THE SOUTH WAS DIFFERENT IN MANY WAYS, BUT OPPRESSION, INTOLERANCE, AND LIMITED OPPORTUNITY WERE PERVASIVE. DISCRIMINATION IN THE WORKPLACE AND HOUSING PERSISTED. THE THREAT OF VIOLENCE WAS EVERYWHERE.

IN WHAT IS KNOWN AS THE RED SUMMER OF 1919, ANGRY WHITE MOBS INSTIGATED MORE THAN 40 RACIALLY MOTIVATED ATTACKS THROUGHOUT THE COUNTRY, KILLING HUNDREDS OF BLACK AMERICANS.

THE SENSELESS VIOLENCE AND KILLING OF THE RED SUMMER WAS NOT THE END OF RACIST TERROR IN AMERICA.

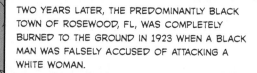

IN 1921, ONE YEAR LATER, THE ALL-BLACK COMMUNITY OF GREENWOOD IN TULSA, OK, WAS ATTACKED BY AN ANGRY WHITE MOB AFTER A WHITE WOMAN ACCUSED A BLACK MAN OF ASSAULTING HER. GREENWOOD, WHICH WAS KNOWN AS "BLACK WALL STREET," WAS DESTROYED.

TWO YEARS LATER, THE PREDOMINANTLY BLACK TOWN OF ROSEWOOD, FL, WAS COMPLETELY BURNED TO THE GROUND IN 1923 WHEN A BLACK MAN WAS FALSELY ACCUSED OF ATTACKING A WHITE WOMAN.

BETWEEN 1882 AND 1968, THERE WERE 3,446 RECORDED LYNCHINGS OF BLACK FOLKS IN THE U.S. IN THE EARLY 1900s, LYNCHINGS HAD BECOME A FORM OF PUBLIC ENTERTAINMENT, WITH POSTCARDS CREATED TO COMMEMORATE THE MURDERS.

FOR DECADES, ACTIVISTS AND POLITICIANS FOUGHT FOR ANTI-LYNCHING LEGISLATION, ONLY TO BE STOPPED AT EVERY TURN BY SOUTHERN POLITICIANS.

THE UNITED STATES CONGRESS WOULD NOT PASS ANY FORM OF ANTI-LYNCHING REGULATION UNTIL 2020--MORE THAN A CENTURY AFTER THE RED SUMMER OF 1919.

MARCUS GARVEY

W. E. B. DU BOIS

WALLACE D. FARD

DISCRIMINATION, OPPRESSION, AND RACIAL VIOLENCE IN THE EARLY 20TH CENTURY GAVE RISE TO A CIVIL RIGHTS MOVEMENT THAT SOUGHT SOCIAL AND POLITICAL EQUALITY FOR BLACK AMERICANS.

THIS TIME WOULD SEE THE BIRTH OF ORGANIZATIONS LIKE THE NATIONAL ASSOCIATION FOR THE ADVANCEMENT OF COLORED PEOPLE (NAACP) AND LEADERS LIKE W. E. B. DU BOIS. IT WOULD ALSO SEE THE BEGINNING OF BLACK NATIONALISM, A MOVEMENT THAT SOUGHT MORE THAN SOCIOPOLITICAL EQUALITY--IT DEMANDED ECONOMIC POWER.

JAMAICAN-BORN MARCUS GARVEY, FOUNDER OF THE UNIVERSAL NEGRO IMPROVEMENT ASSOCIATION, AND WALLACE D. FARD, FOUNDER OF THE NATION OF ISLAM, WERE EARLY EXAMPLES OF BLACK NATIONALISTS WHO ESPOUSED RACIAL PRIDE AND EMPHASIZED THE NEED FOR BLACK FINANCIAL INDEPENDENCE.

BLACK NATIONALISTS LIKE GARVEY CHALLENGED THE ESTABLISHED RACIAL STATUS QUO, AND AS A RESULT WERE SEEN AS A THREAT TO AMERICA, ESPECIALLY BY GOVERNMENT AGENCIES LIKE THE BUREAU OF INVESTIGATION (THE PRECURSOR TO THE FBI), WHICH DEPORTED GARVEY IN 1927.

FOR THOSE SEEKING TO KEEP BLACK AMERICANS IN A PLACE OF OPPRESSION AND INFERIORITY, THERE WOULD BE NO DIFFERENCE BETWEEN CIVIL RIGHTS AND BLACK NATIONALISM--BOTH WERE THREATS TO WHITE SUPREMACY.

AT THE OUTBREAK OF WORLD WAR II, THE EXODUS OF BLACK PEOPLE FROM THE SOUTH INCREASED AS THE NUMBER OF FACTORY JOBS IN THE NORTH AND WEST INCREASED.

DURING THIS SECOND GREAT MIGRATION, BLACK AMERICANS CONTINUED TO ESCAPE THE HORRORS OF THE JIM CROW SOUTH, SEEKING OPPORTUNITY IN THE SO-CALLED PROGRESSIVE STATES IN THE NORTH AND WEST.

MEANWHILE, MORE THAN 100,000 BLACK SERVICEMEN WERE DEPLOYED OVERSEAS DURING WWII. BUT AS THEY FOUGHT FOR FREEDOM IN OTHER PARTS OF THE WORLD, THEY WERE SERVING IN A SEGREGATED MILITARY.

AND WHEN BLACK SOLDIERS RETURNED HOME AFTER THE WAR, THEY RETURNED TO A COUNTRY WHERE THEY WERE STILL NOT EQUAL.

COLORED WAITING ROOM

BLACK PEOPLE HAD BEEN FIGHTING FOR EQUALITY AND JUSTICE LONG BEFORE THE CIVIL RIGHTS MOVEMENT BEGAN IN THE 1950s.

A MAJOR VICTORY CAME IN 1954, WHEN THE U.S. SUPREME COURT RULED IN *BROWN V. BOARD OF EDUCATION* THAT RACIAL SEGREGATION IN PUBLIC SCHOOLS WAS UNCONSTITUTIONAL. THIS LANDMARK RULING HELPED TO LAUNCH WHAT IS GENERALLY THOUGHT OF AS THE CIVIL RIGHTS MOVEMENT.

The News

HIGH COURT BANS SEGREGATION IN PUBLIC SCHOOLS

SAVE SEGREGATION VOTE STATES RIGHTS

SAVE SEGREGATION VOTE STATES RIGHTS

THE DESEGREGATION OF AMERICAN SCHOOLS DID NOT COME EASILY. RESISTANCE TO DESEGREGATION WAS OFTEN VIOLENT.

IN ARKANSAS, GOVERNOR ORVAL FAUBUS REFUSED TO ALLOW NINE STUDENTS—THE LITTLE ROCK NINE—TO ATTEND LITTLE ROCK CENTRAL HIGH SCHOOL IN 1957.

IN RESPONSE TO THREATS MADE AGAINST THE LITTLE ROCK NINE, PRESIDENT DWIGHT D. EISENHOWER DEPLOYED THE 101ST AIRBORNE DIVISION OF THE U.S. ARMY TO PROTECT THEM.

IN 1960, 6-YEAR-OLD RUBY BRIDGES, THE FIRST BLACK STUDENT TO ATTEND WILLIAM FRANTZ ELEMENTARY SCHOOL IN NEW ORLEANS, HAD TO BE ESCORTED INTO SCHOOL BY U.S. MARSHALS. THE SAME WAS TRUE FOR LEONA TATE, TESSIE PREVOST, AND GAIL ETIENNE (THE McDONOGH THREE), A TRIO OF 6-YEAR-OLDS THREATENED AS THEY USHERED IN DESEGREGATION AT THEIR SCHOOL.

IN A SCENE THAT WAS BECOMING INCREASINGLY FAMILIAR IN SOUTHERN STATES, U.S. MARSHALS WERE ALSO SENT TO PROTECT JAMES MEREDITH AS HE ENROLLED AT THE UNIVERSITY OF MISSISSIPPI IN 1961.

WE WANT TO KEEP OUR SCHOOL WHITE

THE STRUGGLE TO INTEGRATE SCHOOLS IN THE SOUTH WAS ONE OF THE MOST CRUCIAL PARTS OF THE CIVIL RIGHTS MOVEMENT, BECAUSE SEGREGATION IN SCHOOLS WAS A CLEAR AND VISIBLE REPRESENTATION OF RACIAL INEQUALITY PLAGUING AMERICA.

AUGUST 28, 1955. EMMETT TILL, A 14-YEAR-OLD FROM CHICAGO, WAS VISITING RELATIVES IN MONEY, MS, WHEN HE WAS ACCUSED OF WHISTLING AT A WHITE WOMAN.

THAT NIGHT, HE WAS DRAGGED FROM THE HOME OF HIS UNCLE AND BRUTALLY MURDERED. THREE DAYS LATER, HIS MUTILATED BODY WAS FOUND IN THE TALLAHATCHIE RIVER.

TILL'S BODY WAS RETURNED TO CHICAGO FOR BURIAL. HIS MOTHER, MAMIE TILL-MOBLEY, INSISTED ON AN OPEN CASKET BECAUSE SHE WANTED THE WORLD TO SEE WHAT HAD HAPPENED TO HER SON. PHOTOS OF TILL'S HORRIFICALLY DISFIGURED CORPSE APPEARED IN NEWSPAPERS AND MAGAZINES ALL OVER THE COUNTRY.

THE MURDER OF EMMETT TILL NOT ONLY SHED LIGHT ON THE HORRORS OF RACISM IN AMERICA, IT SERVED AS A RALLYING CRY FOR THE CIVIL RIGHTS MOVEMENT.

LESS THAN SIX MONTHS AFTER THE MURDER OF EMMETT TILL, ROSA PARKS REFUSED TO GIVE UP HER SEAT ON A SEGREGATED BUS IN MONTGOMERY, AL.

THOUGH PARKS'S ACTIONS BECAME THE CATALYST FOR ONE OF THE MOST CRUCIAL MOMENTS OF THE CIVIL RIGHTS MOVEMENT--THE MONTGOMERY BUS BOYCOTT--SHE WAS NOT THE FIRST PERSON TO PERFORM THE ACT OF PROTEST ON A BUS.

AND NINE YEARS BEFORE THAT, ON JULY 16, 1944, IRENE MORGAN WAS ARRESTED FOR REFUSING TO GIVE UP HER SEAT ON A BUS TRAVELING FROM MARYLAND, WHERE THERE WAS NO SEGREGATION ON BUSES, TO VIRGINIA, WHERE THERE WAS.

MORGAN'S CASE LED TO THE SUPREME COURT DECISION IN *MORGAN V. VIRGINIA*, WHICH RULED THAT SEGREGATION ON INTERSTATE BUSES WAS UNCONSTITUTIONAL.

NINE MONTHS BEFORE ROSA PARKS, 15-YEAR-OLD CLAUDETTE COLVIN WAS ARRESTED FOR REFUSING TO GIVE UP HER SEAT IN THE FRONT OF A BUS IN MONTGOMERY.

CLEVELAND AVE.

ALONG WITH SEGREGATION IN SCHOOLS, SEGREGATION ON BUSES WAS A HUGE PART OF THE CIVIL RIGHTS MOVEMENT BECAUSE BOTH ISSUES LED TO COURT RULINGS THAT PROVIDED LEGAL PRECEDENTS FOR DESEGREGATION.

THE SUPREME COURT DECISIONS TO DESEGREGATE SCHOOLS AND INTERSTATE BUS TRAVEL BECAME KEY RALLYING POINTS IN THE GROWING CIVIL RIGHTS MOVEMENT. AMID THE GROWING FIGHT FOR EQUALITY, CIVIL RIGHTS ORGANIZATIONS BEGAN TO FORM. ONE SUCH ORGANIZATION WAS THE SOUTHERN CHRISTIAN LEADERSHIP CONFERENCE (SCLC), AND ITS MOST RECOGNIZABLE MEMBER WAS DR. MARTIN LUTHER KING, JR.

AS THE CIVIL RIGHTS MOVEMENT GREW, DR. KING BECAME ITS LEADING SPOKESPERSON. HE WAS A POWERFUL SPEAKER AND A CHARISMATIC LEADER WHO BELIEVED ANY SORT OF VIOLENCE WOULD BE COUNTERPRODUCTIVE TO THE STRUGGLE FOR EQUALITY.

DR. MARTIN LUTHER KING, JR.

CORETTA SCOTT KING

RALPH ABERNATHY

FRED SHUTTLESWORTH

ELLA BAKER

BAYARD RUSTIN

A. PHILIP RANDOLPH

DESPITE THE COMMITMENT TO NONVIOLENCE MADE BY DR. KING AND OTHER MEMBERS OF THE CIVIL RIGHTS MOVEMENT, THE RACIST OPPOSITION TO DESEGREGATION DID NOT PRACTICE NONVIOLENCE.

ON SEPTEMBER 15, 1963, MEMBERS OF THE WHITE SUPREMACIST HATE GROUP THE KU KLUX KLAN (KKK) BOMBED THE 16TH STREET BAPTIST CHURCH IN BIRMINGHAM, AL, KILLING 11-YEAR-OLD CAROL DENISE McNAIR, AND THREE 14-YEAR-OLDS, ADDIE MAE COLLINS, CYNTHIA WESLEY, AND CAROLE ROBERTSON.

NO ONE WAS HELD RESPONSIBLE FOR THE KILLINGS FOR MORE THAN TEN YEARS.

THREE MONTHS BEFORE THE BOMBING OF THE 16TH STREET BAPTIST CHURCH, CIVIL RIGHTS LEADER MEDGAR EVERS WAS ASSASSINATED IN FRONT OF HIS HOUSE BY WHITE SUPREMACIST BYRON DE LA BECKWITH.

IT WOULD TAKE MORE THAN 30 YEARS FOR DE LA BECKWITH TO BE CONVICTED OF THE MURDER.

ANDREW GOODMAN, JAMES CHANEY, AND MICHAEL SCHWERNER WERE CIVIL RIGHTS ACTIVISTS WORKING TO REGISTER VOTERS IN MISSISSIPPI. ALL THREE WERE KILLED BY A GROUP OF WHITE SUPREMACISTS ON JUNE 21, 1964.

THEY WERE NOT THE ONLY VICTIMS OF FATAL RACIST ATTACKS. BETWEEN 1955 AND 1968, THERE WERE 41 CIVIL RIGHTS MARTYRS KILLED IN VIOLENT ATTACKS.

REV. GEORGE LEE (51).
MAY 7, 1955.

LAMAR SMITH (63).
AUGUST 13, 1955.

JOHN EARL REESE (16).
OCTOBER 22, 1955.

WILLIE EDWARDS, JR. (24).
JANUARY 23, 1957.

MACK CHARLES PARKER
(23). APRIL 25, 1959.

HERBERT LEE (49).
SEPTEMBER 25, 1961.

ROMAN DUCKSWORTH, JR.
(28). APRIL 9, 1962.

PAUL GUIHARD (31).
SEPTEMBER 30, 1962.

WILLIAM LEWIS MOORE (35).
APRIL 23, 1963.

VIRGIL LAMAR WARE (13).
SEPTEMBER 15, 1963.

LOUIS ALLEN (44).
JANUARY 31, 1964.

JOHNNIE MAE CHAPPELL
(35). MARCH 23, 1964.

REV. BRUCE KLUNDER (26).
APRIL 7, 1964.

HENRY HEZEKIAH DEE (19).
MAY 2, 1964.

CHARLES EDDIE MOORE
(20). MAY 2, 1964.

LEMUEL PENN (48).
JULY 11, 1964.

JIMMIE LEE JACKSON (26). FEBRUARY 26, 1965.

REV. JAMES REEB (38). MARCH 11, 1965.

VIOLA GREGG LIUZZO (39). MARCH 25, 1965.

ONEAL MOORE (34). JUNE 2, 1965.

WILLIE WALLACE BREWSTER (38). JULY 18, 1965.

JONATHAN MYRICK DANIELS (26). AUGUST 20, 1965.

SAMUEL YOUNGE, JR. (21). JANUARY 3, 1966.

VERNON DAHMER (57). JANUARY 10, 1966.

BEN CHESTER WHITE (67). JUNE 10, 1966.

CLARENCE TRIGGS (76). JULY 30, 1966.

WHARLEST JACKSON (37). FEBRUARY 27, 1967.

BENJAMIN BROWN (22). MAY 12, 1967.

SAMUEL HAMMOND, JR. (18). FEBRUARY 8, 1968.

DELANO MIDDLETON (17). FEBRUARY 8, 1968.

HENRY SMITH (19). FEBRUARY 8, 1968.

IN ADDITION TO THE 41 MARTYRS RECOGNIZED BY THE CIVIL RIGHTS MEMORIAL IN MONTGOMERY, AL, THERE ARE ANOTHER 74 NAMES LISTED OF PEOPLE KILLED IN CONNECTION WITH THE MOVEMENT.

THE VIOLENT OPPOSITION TO CIVIL RIGHTS LED MANY TO QUESTION THE VALIDITY OF NONVIOLENCE. IN THE LATE 1950s, ROBERT F. WILLIAMS FORMED THE BLACK ARMED GUARD IN NORTH CAROLINA, AN ORGANIZATION DEDICATED TO PROTECTING CIVIL RIGHTS ACTIVISTS AGAINST RACIST ATTACKS.

WILLIAMS AND HIS ORGANIZATION TRADED SHOTS WITH THE KKK, AND IN 1961 HE RELOCATED TO CUBA, WHERE HE BROADCAST THE RADIO PROGRAM "RADIO FREE DIXIE" TO THE SOUTHERN UNITED STATES. IN 1962, HE PUBLISHED HIS BOOK, *NEGROES WITH GUNS*.

IN NOVEMBER 1964, EARNEST "CHILLY WILLY" THOMAS AND FREDERICK DOUGLASS KIRKPATRICK FORMED THE DEACONS FOR DEFENSE AND JUSTICE IN JONESBORO, LA.

WITHIN A YEAR, THERE WOULD BE MORE CHAPTERS OF THE DEACONS IN LOUISIANA, ALABAMA, AND MISSISSIPPI. THE ARMED ORGANIZATION WORKED WITH NONVIOLENT CIVIL RIGHTS GROUPS, PROVIDING SECURITY AT MARCHES AND RALLIES. THE PROTECTION OF THE DEACONS ALLOWED ORGANIZATIONS LIKE THE NAACP TO MAINTAIN THEIR PRACTICE OF NONVIOLENCE.

IN REJECTING NONVIOLENCE, MALCOLM X BECAME ONE OF THE MOST CONTROVERSIAL LEADERS OF THE CIVIL RIGHTS MOVEMENT, FIRST AS A MEMBER OF THE NATION OF ISLAM FROM 1952 TO 1964, AND THEN AS THE FOUNDER OF THE ORGANIZATION OF AFRO-AMERICAN UNITY.

I DON'T FAVOR VIOLENCE. IF WE COULD BRING ABOUT RECOGNITION AND RESPECT OF OUR PEOPLE BY PEACEFUL MEANS, WELL AND GOOD. EVERYBODY WOULD LIKE TO REACH HIS OBJECTIVES PEACEFULLY.

BUT I'M ALSO A REALIST. THE ONLY PEOPLE IN THIS COUNTRY WHO ARE ASKED TO BE NONVIOLENT ARE BLACK PEOPLE.

THE STUDENT NONVIOLENT COORDINATING COMMITTEE (SNCC) FORMED IN 1960, GROWING OUT OF SEVERAL SUCCESSFUL SIT-INS PROTESTING SEGREGATION IN DEPARTMENT STORES IN NORTH CAROLINA AND TENNESSEE.

COMPRISED MOSTLY OF COLLEGE-AGE MEMBERS, SNCC WORKED DIRECTLY WITH OTHER ORGANIZATIONS SUCH AS THE NAACP AND SCLC. HOWEVER, SNCC'S EVOLVING IDEOLOGY SET IT APART FROM OTHER ORGANIZATIONS THAT WERE MORE CONSERVATIVE.

SNCC MEMBERS WERE CRUCIAL PARTICIPANTS IN MANY OF THE MOST IMPORTANT CIVIL RIGHTS CAMPAIGNS, INCLUDING THE FREEDOM RIDES OF 1961, THE MARCH ON WASHINGTON IN 1963, THE FREEDOM SUMMER OF 1964, AND THE SELMA TO MONTGOMERY MARCHES OF 1965.

STOKELY CARMICHAEL WAS A KEY MEMBER OF SNCC, AND HE HAD WITNESSED MANY ATTACKS ON NONVIOLENT PROTESTERS. BORN IN 1941, CARMICHAEL WAS YOUNGER THAN MANY OF THE OTHER CIVIL RIGHTS LEADERS, LESS PATIENT, AND INCREASINGLY SKEPTICAL OF THE STRATEGY OF NONVIOLENCE.

MEMBERS OF SNCC WENT TO LOWNDES COUNTY, AL, TO HELP WITH VOTER REGISTRATION IN 1965. ALSO KNOWN AS "BLOODY LOWNDES," THE COUNTY WAS 80% BLACK, BUT THE KKK DENIED VOTING RIGHTS TO BLACK CITIZENS THROUGH INTIMIDATION AND VIOLENCE.

THE THREAT OF VIOLENCE FROM THE KKK WAS CONSTANT IN LOWNDES COUNTY. AS A RESULT, MOST OF THE BLACK RESIDENTS CARRIED GUNS FOR PROTECTION, WHICH WAS IN DIRECT CONTRADICTION TO THE NONVIOLENT STANCE OF SNCC AND OTHER MAJOR CIVIL RIGHTS ORGANIZATIONS.

IT WAS IN LOWNDES COUNTY THAT STOKELY CARMICHAEL AND OTHER MEMBERS OF SNCC BEGAN TO RECONSIDER THEIR POSITION ON NONVIOLENCE.

SNCC WORKED WITH THE BLACK CITIZENS TO FORM AN INDEPENDENT POLITICAL PARTY KNOWN AS THE LOWNDES COUNTY FREEDOM ORGANIZATION (LCFO), RATHER THAN JOINING THE LOCAL DEMOCRATIC PARTY, WHICH WAS LED BY SEGREGATIONISTS.

THE LCFO ADOPTED AS ITS MASCOT A BLACK PANTHER--A SYMBOL OF STRENGTH AND POWER THAT WAS A STARK CONTRAST TO THE WHITE ROOSTER USED AS A MASCOT FOR THE REGIONAL DEMOCRATS. IN TIME, THE LCFO WOULD BECOME KNOWN AS THE BLACK PANTHER PARTY.

ON AUGUST 11, 1965, LOS ANGELES POLICE OFFICERS PULLED OVER BLACK MOTORIST MARQUETTE FRYE, LEADING TO AN ALTERCATION THAT WOULD SET OFF THE MASSIVE WATTS UPRISING.

OVER THE COURSE OF SIX DAYS, LOOTING, RIOTING, AND VIOLENCE DEVASTATED THE LARGELY BLACK LOS ANGELES NEIGHBORHOOD OF WATTS. THE NATIONAL GUARD WAS DEPLOYED TO TRY TO CURB THE VIOLENCE, MORE THAN 3,000 PEOPLE WERE ARRESTED, AND MORE THAN 30 PEOPLE WERE KILLED.

THE WATTS UPRISING SERVED AS NOTICE THAT THE RACIAL PROBLEMS PLAGUING AMERICA WERE NOT LIMITED TO SOUTHERN STATES. LOS ANGELES, LIKE MANY CITIES ACROSS THE COUNTRY, HAD A LONG HISTORY OF RACIAL INJUSTICE.

IN THE WAKE OF THE WATTS UPRISING, CALIFORNIA GOVERNOR PAT BROWN ORDERED AN INVESTIGATION LED BY THE McCONE COMMISSION TO DETERMINE THE CAUSE OF THE RIOT.

IN A REPORT CALLED "VIOLENCE IN THE CITY—AN END OR A BEGINNING?: A REPORT BY THE GOVERNOR'S COMMISSION ON THE LOS ANGELES RIOTS, 1965," THE McCONE COMMISSION DETERMINED THAT THE ROOT CAUSES WERE HIGH UNEMPLOYMENT, INFERIOR SCHOOLS, BAD POLICE RELATIONS, AND POOR LIVING CONDITIONS IN THE BLACK COMMUNITIES OF LOS ANGELES. RECOMMENDATIONS TO ADDRESS THE CAUSES OF THE RIOT WENT UNHEEDED.

BY 1965, AMERICA WAS EMBROILED IN THE VIETNAM WAR. THE U.S. MILITARY WAS NO LONGER SEGREGATED, AND MORE BLACK SOLDIERS SERVED IN VIETNAM THAN ANY OTHER WAR IN AMERICAN HISTORY. NEARLY 25% OF AMERICAN SOLDIERS KILLED IN VIETNAM IN 1965 WERE BLACK.

THE UNPOPULARITY OF THE WAR CONTRIBUTED TO THE POLITICAL TURMOIL IN AMERICA. FOR MANY BLACK AMERICANS, THE WAR IN VIETNAM—A WAR FOR "FREEDOM"— WAS ESPECIALLY PROBLEMATIC, GIVEN THE ONGOING STRUGGLE FOR EQUALITY AND JUSTICE IN THE U.S.

IN 1966, WORLD HEAVYWEIGHT BOXING CHAMPION MUHAMMAD ALI REFUSED TO BE DRAFTED INTO THE MILITARY, CITING HIS OPPOSITION TO THE WAR.

ALI WAS JUST ONE OF MANY BLACK AMERICANS TAKING A STAND AGAINST THE WAR, CALLING INTO QUESTION AMERICA'S HYPOCRISY WHEN IT CAME TO THEIR FREEDOM.

WHY SHOULD THEY ASK ME TO PUT ON A UNIFORM AND GO 10,000 MILES FROM HOME AND DROP BOMBS AND BULLETS ON BROWN PEOPLE IN VIETNAM WHILE SO-CALLED NEGRO PEOPLE IN LOUISVILLE ARE TREATED LIKE DOGS AND DENIED SIMPLE HUMAN RIGHTS?

NO, I AM NOT GOING 10,000 MILES FROM HOME TO HELP MURDER AND BURN ANOTHER POOR NATION SIMPLY TO CONTINUE THE DOMINATION OF WHITE SLAVE MASTERS OF THE DARKER PEOPLE THE WORLD OVER.

THE WATTS UPRISING OF 1965 PROVED TO BE THE PRECURSOR FOR WHAT WAS TO COME IN 1966. MORE THAN TEN CITIES ERUPTED IN VIOLENCE--ALL IN RESPONSE TO POLICE ACTIONS.

ON JUNE 5, 1966, CIVIL RIGHTS ACTIVIST JAMES MEREDITH SET OUT ON WHAT HE CALLED THE MARCH AGAINST FEAR--A 220-MILE MARCH FROM MEMPHIS, TN, TO JACKSON, MS.

MEREDITH PLANNED TO MARCH ALONE AS AN ACT OF PROTEST AGAINST RACISM, AND TO ENCOURAGE VOTER REGISTRATION.

DURING HIS SECOND DAY ON THE ROAD, MEREDITH WAS SHOT BY A SNIPER.

WITH MEREDITH IN THE HOSPITAL, OTHER CIVIL RIGHTS ACTIVISTS AND ORGANIZATIONS CARRIED ON WITH HIS CAUSE, INCLUDING SNCC AND STOKELY CARMICHAEL.

ON JUNE 16, 1966, CARMICHAEL GAVE A POWERFUL SPEECH TO A LARGE CROWD IN GREENWOOD, MS.

WE BEEN SAYING "FREEDOM" FOR SIX YEARS NOW, AND WE AIN'T GOT NOTHING!

WHAT WE GOT TO START SAYING NOW IS "*BLACK POWER*"!

WE WANT *BLACK POWER*!

IT WAS AT THIS POINT THAT CARMICHAEL FORMALLY DISTANCED HIMSELF AND SNCC FROM THE NONVIOLENT MOVEMENT, AND THE BLACK POWER MOVEMENT WAS BORN.

THREE — 1966: Birth of the Panthers

AMID THE PROTESTING, MARCHING, AND VIOLENCE, BLACK PEOPLE ALL ACROSS AMERICA LOOKED FOR A WAY TO MAKE A DIFFERENCE.

IN OAKLAND, CA, BOBBY SEALE AND HUEY P. NEWTON FOUNDED THE BLACK PANTHER PARTY FOR SELF-DEFENSE IN OCTOBER 1966.

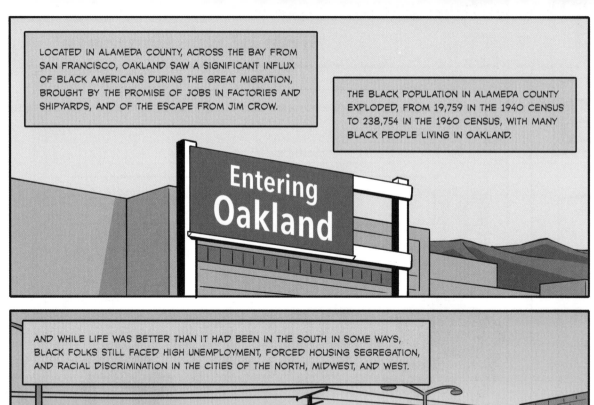

LOCATED IN ALAMEDA COUNTY, ACROSS THE BAY FROM SAN FRANCISCO, OAKLAND SAW A SIGNIFICANT INFLUX OF BLACK AMERICANS DURING THE GREAT MIGRATION, BROUGHT BY THE PROMISE OF JOBS IN FACTORIES AND SHIPYARDS, AND OF THE ESCAPE FROM JIM CROW.

THE BLACK POPULATION IN ALAMEDA COUNTY EXPLODED, FROM 19,759 IN THE 1940 CENSUS TO 238,754 IN THE 1960 CENSUS, WITH MANY BLACK PEOPLE LIVING IN OAKLAND.

Entering
Oakland

AND WHILE LIFE WAS BETTER THAN IT HAD BEEN IN THE SOUTH IN SOME WAYS, BLACK FOLKS STILL FACED HIGH UNEMPLOYMENT, FORCED HOUSING SEGREGATION, AND RACIAL DISCRIMINATION IN THE CITIES OF THE NORTH, MIDWEST, AND WEST.

THIS WAS ESPECIALLY TRUE IN OAKLAND. MOST OF THE SHIPYARD AND FACTORY JOBS HAD GONE AWAY AFTER WWII, AND POVERTY DEVASTATED THE BLACK COMMUNITY.

MAKING MATTERS WORSE, OAKLAND HAD A BAD REPUTATION FOR POLICE BRUTALITY AND CORRUPTION. MANY OF THE POLICE OFFICERS WERE WHITE MEN WHO HAD BEEN RECRUITED FROM THE SOUTH OR WHOSE FAMILIES HAD RELOCATED FROM SOUTHERN STATES DURING WWII.

THE OAKLAND POLICE DEPARTMENT WAS 96% WHITE IN 1966, WHILE THE CITY ITSELF WAS NEARLY 50% NONWHITE.

Mark Comfort

THERE WERE MANY INFLUENCES IN THE CREATION OF THE BLACK PANTHER PARTY FOR SELF-DEFENSE, BUT PERHAPS NONE MORE CRUCIAL THAN MARK COMFORT, A COMMUNITY ACTIVIST AND VIETNAM WAR VETERAN FROM OAKLAND.

COMFORT HAD SPENT TIME WORKING SECURITY IN LOWNDES COUNTY WITH STOKELY CARMICHAEL, SNCC, AND THE LCFO. INSPIRED BY WHAT HE HAD SEEN IN LOWNDES, COMFORT RETURNED TO CALIFORNIA IN 1965 TO FOUND THE OAKLAND DIRECT ACTION COMMITTEE (ODAC), AN ORGANIZATION DEDICATED TO SERVING THE NEEDS OF POOR PEOPLE IN THE COMMUNITY.

BY EARLY 1966, COMFORT AND MEMBERS OF ODAC WERE PATROLLING THE STREETS OF OAKLAND TO PROTECT THE BLACK COMMUNITY FROM POLICE BRUTALITY. FOR A TIME, COMFORT WOULD FOLLOW POLICE AFTER THEY TOOK A SUSPECT INTO CUSTODY, AND THEN POST BAIL FOR THE INDIVIDUAL WHO HAD BEEN ARRESTED.

COMFORT WAS THE DIRECT LINK BETWEEN THE LOWNDES COUNTY BLACK PANTHER PARTY AND THE PANTHERS THAT WOULD FORM IN OAKLAND. ALTHOUGH HE NEVER OFFICIALLY JOINED THE GROUP, COMFORT'S ORGANIZATION, ODAC, WAS A DIRECT INSPIRATION FOR WHAT WOULD BECOME THE BLACK PANTHER PARTY FOR SELF-DEFENSE.

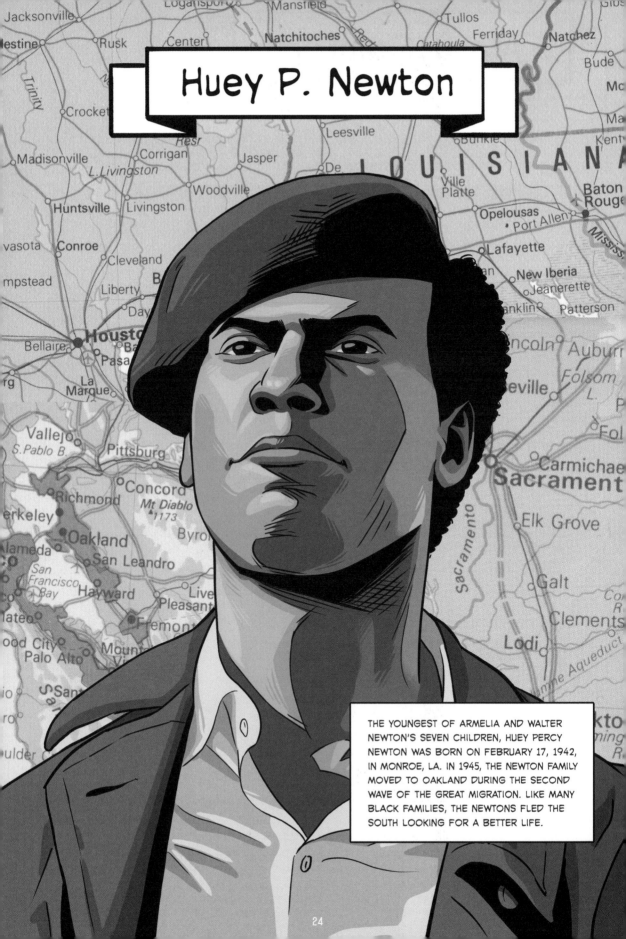

Huey P. Newton

THE YOUNGEST OF ARMELIA AND WALTER NEWTON'S SEVEN CHILDREN, HUEY PERCY NEWTON WAS BORN ON FEBRUARY 17, 1942, IN MONROE, LA. IN 1945, THE NEWTON FAMILY MOVED TO OAKLAND DURING THE SECOND WAVE OF THE GREAT MIGRATION. LIKE MANY BLACK FAMILIES, THE NEWTONS FLED THE SOUTH LOOKING FOR A BETTER LIFE.

HUEY NEWTON STRUGGLED IN SCHOOL, AND BY THE TIME HE WAS IN HIGH SCHOOL, HE STILL COULD NOT READ OR WRITE. MUCH OF HIS TIME WAS SPENT ON THE STREETS, FOLLOWING IN THE FOOTSTEPS OF TWO OF HIS OLDER BROTHERS, WHO WERE PETTY CRIMINALS. WHILE IN HIGH SCHOOL, A COUNSELOR TOLD NEWTON THAT HE WAS NOT MEANT FOR COLLEGE AND WOULD DO NOTHING OF IMPORTANCE WITH HIS LIFE. NEWTON DECIDED TO PROVE HIM WRONG.

NEWTON LEARNED TO READ AND WRITE, GRADUATED FROM HIGH SCHOOL IN 1959, AND BEGAN ATTENDING MERRITT COLLEGE IN OAKLAND. HE EXPANDED HIS MIND BY READING THE WORKS OF W. E. B. DU BOIS AND FRANTZ FANON, AS WELL AS BOOKS LIKE RALPH ELLISON'S *INVISIBLE MAN* AND JAMES BALDWIN'S *THE FIRE NEXT TIME.*

AT MERRITT, NEWTON MET ACTIVIST DONALD WARDEN, BECOMING INVOLVED IN THE COLLEGE'S AFRO-AMERICAN ASSOCIATION. NEWTON COULD OFTEN BE FOUND DEBATING ON AND AROUND CAMPUS. AT THE SAME TIME, HE WAS LEADING SOMETHING OF A DOUBLE LIFE.

WHILE STUDYING LAW BY DAY, NEWTON LED THE LIFE OF A SMALL-TIME CRIMINAL AT NIGHT. IN HIS OWN WORDS, "I STUDIED LAW TO BECOME A BETTER BURGLAR."

IT WAS AT MERRITT COLLEGE THAT NEWTON MET BOBBY SEALE.

Bobby Seale

THE OLDEST OF GEORGE AND THELMA SEALE'S THREE CHILDREN, BOBBY SEALE WAS BORN ON OCTOBER 22, 1936, IN LIBERTY, TX. THE SEALE FAMILY RELOCATED FROM TEXAS TO CALIFORNIA IN 1944.

RAISED BY AN ABUSIVE FATHER, SEALE WAS NO STRANGER TO VIOLENCE, AND HE DID NOT FEAR CONFRONTATION. AS A CHILD, HE BECAME KNOWN FOR STANDING UP TO BULLIES, EVEN IF IT MEANT TAKING A BEATING.

SEALE DROPPED OUT OF HIGH SCHOOL AND JOINED THE AIR FORCE IN 1955. THREE YEARS AFTER ENLISTING, HE WAS GIVEN A DISHONORABLE DISCHARGE FOR FIGHTING.

BACK IN OAKLAND BUT UNABLE TO FIND STABLE EMPLOYMENT, SEALE RETURNED TO SCHOOL IN 1960 TO GET HIS HIGH SCHOOL DIPLOMA. HE THEN ENROLLED AT MERRITT COLLEGE, STUDYING ENGINEERING AND POLITICS.

IN 1962, SEALE MET HUEY NEWTON AT MERRITT WHEN NEWTON WAS LEADING A DEMONSTRATION PROTESTING THE BLOCKADE OF CUBA.

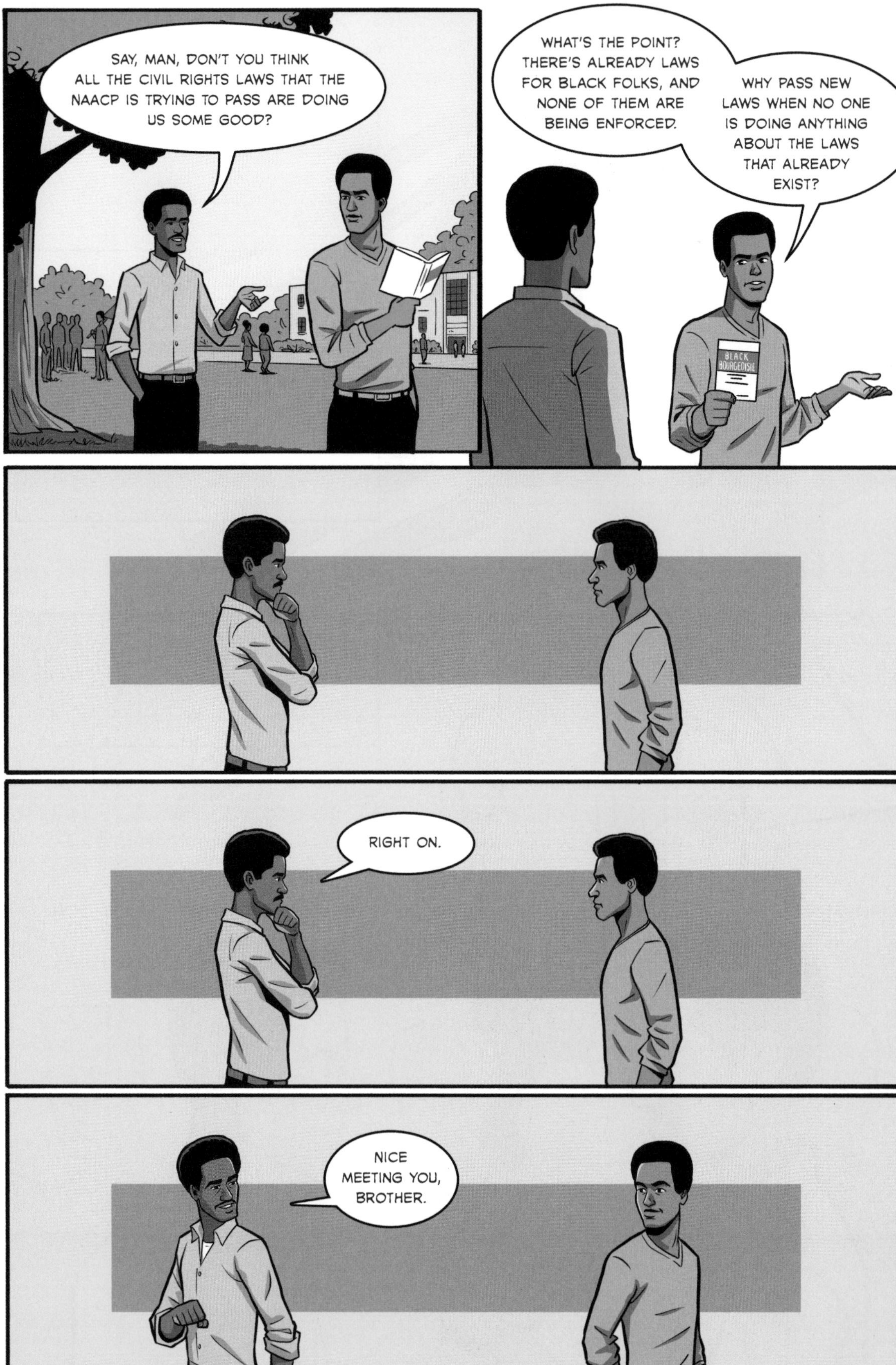
SAY, MAN, DON'T YOU THINK ALL THE CIVIL RIGHTS LAWS THAT THE NAACP IS TRYING TO PASS ARE DOING US SOME GOOD?
WHAT'S THE POINT? THERE'S ALREADY LAWS FOR BLACK FOLKS, AND NONE OF THEM ARE BEING ENFORCED.
WHY PASS NEW LAWS WHEN NO ONE IS DOING ANYTHING ABOUT THE LAWS THAT ALREADY EXIST?
BLACK BOURGEOISIE
RIGHT ON.
NICE MEETING YOU, BROTHER.

THOUGH THEY HAD HIT IT OFF, SEALE AND NEWTON WERE LEADING VERY DIFFERENT LIVES.

SEALE CONTINUED TO WORK AND GO TO SCHOOL WHILE LOOKING FOR A WAY TO FIGHT THE RACIAL INJUSTICES FACED BY BLACK FOLKS IN AMERICA.

BY 1964, HE HAD BECOME MORE POLITICALLY INVOLVED WITH ORGANIZATIONS LIKE REVOLUTIONARY ACTION MOVEMENT (RAM), AN ORGANIZATION ROOTED IN BLACK NATIONALISM.

MEANWHILE, NEWTON WAS IN JAIL, SERVING A SIX-MONTH SENTENCE FOR ASSAULT.

SPENDING A CONSIDERABLE AMOUNT OF TIME IN SOLITARY CONFINEMENT, NEWTON STRUGGLED TO KEEP FROM LOSING HIS MIND, AND IN THE PROCESS FOUND AN INNER STRENGTH THAT ALLOWED HIM TO ENDURE.

ON FEBRUARY 21, 1965, MALCOLM X WAS ASSASSINATED.

MALCOLM X WAS A PERSONAL HERO OF SEALE'S, AND HIS MURDER FILLED SEALE WITH RAGE.

OVERCOME WITH ANGER AND GRIEF AND NOT KNOWING WHAT ELSE TO DO, SEALE STOOD ON A STREET CORNER, THROWING BRICKS AT PASSING CARS.

BEFORE HE COULD GET INTO SERIOUS TROUBLE, SEALE'S COMPANIONS FROM RAM CAME TO FIND HIM AND TRY TO CALM HIM DOWN.

BUT SEALE DIDN'T WANT TO BE CALM. HE WANTED TO FIGHT--SOMETHING THE MEMBERS OF RAM WERE NOT INTERESTED IN DOING. FOR A GROUP CALLED REVOLUTIONARY ACTION MOVEMENT, THE TERM "REVOLUTIONARY" WAS LARGELY INTELLECTUAL.

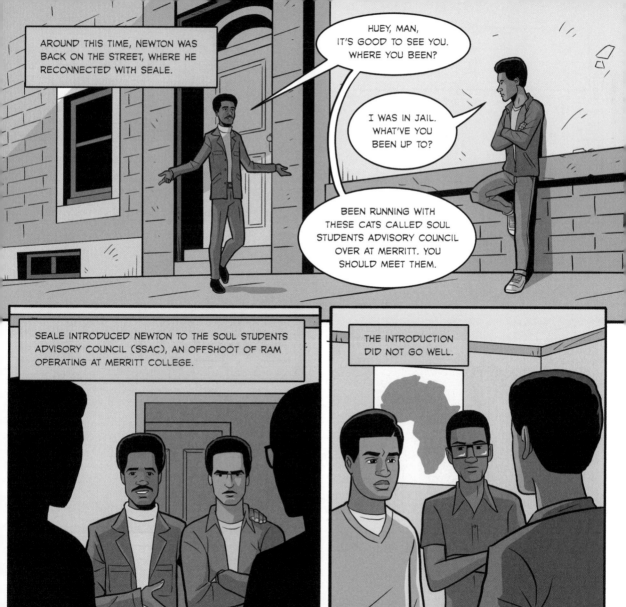

AROUND THIS TIME, NEWTON WAS BACK ON THE STREET, WHERE HE RECONNECTED WITH SEALE.

HUEY, MAN, IT'S GOOD TO SEE YOU. WHERE YOU BEEN?

I WAS IN JAIL. WHAT'VE YOU BEEN UP TO?

BEEN RUNNING WITH THESE CATS CALLED SOUL STUDENTS ADVISORY COUNCIL OVER AT MERRITT. YOU SHOULD MEET THEM.

SEALE INTRODUCED NEWTON TO THE SOUL STUDENTS ADVISORY COUNCIL (SSAC), AN OFFSHOOT OF RAM OPERATING AT MERRITT COLLEGE.

THE INTRODUCTION DID NOT GO WELL.

MAN, THOSE CATS ARE JIVE--AIN'T A THING REVOLUTIONARY ABOUT THEM.

THEY'RE ARMCHAIR REVOLUTIONARIES. MAYBE WE NEED TO START OUR OWN THING.

NEWTON AND SEALE BEGAN SPENDING MORE TIME TOGETHER, TALKING ABOUT WHAT THEY BELIEVED AND WHAT THEY WANTED TO DO.

BOB'S

AT THIS TIME, THEY WEREN'T DOING MUCH MORE THAN TALKING--NOT TOO DIFFERENT FROM THE ARMCHAIR REVOLUTIONARIES THEY DISLIKED.

WHILE IN COLLEGE, SEALE HAD EARNED MONEY AS A STAND-UP COMEDIAN AND ACTOR, EARNING A REPUTATION AS A PERFORMER. ON MARCH 17, 1966, WHILE HANGING OUT WITH NEWTON IN BERKELEY, CA, SEALE BEGAN TO RECITE AN ANTI-WAR POEM.

THE POLICE ARRIVED, CLAIMING THAT SEALE WAS DISTURBING THE PEACE, AND ARRESTED BOTH SEALE AND NEWTON.

STUCK IN JAIL WITH NO MONEY, NEWTON AND SEALE HAD TO CALL THE SSAC TO BAIL THEM OUT.

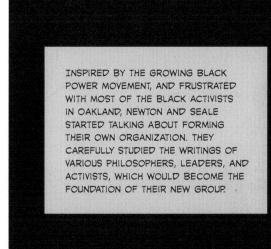

INSPIRED BY THE GROWING BLACK POWER MOVEMENT, AND FRUSTRATED WITH MOST OF THE BLACK ACTIVISTS IN OAKLAND, NEWTON AND SEALE STARTED TALKING ABOUT FORMING THEIR OWN ORGANIZATION. THEY CAREFULLY STUDIED THE WRITINGS OF VARIOUS PHILOSOPHERS, LEADERS, AND ACTIVISTS, WHICH WOULD BECOME THE FOUNDATION OF THEIR NEW GROUP.

FRANTZ FANON

MALCOLM X

KARL MARX

MAO ZEDONG

CHE GUEVARA

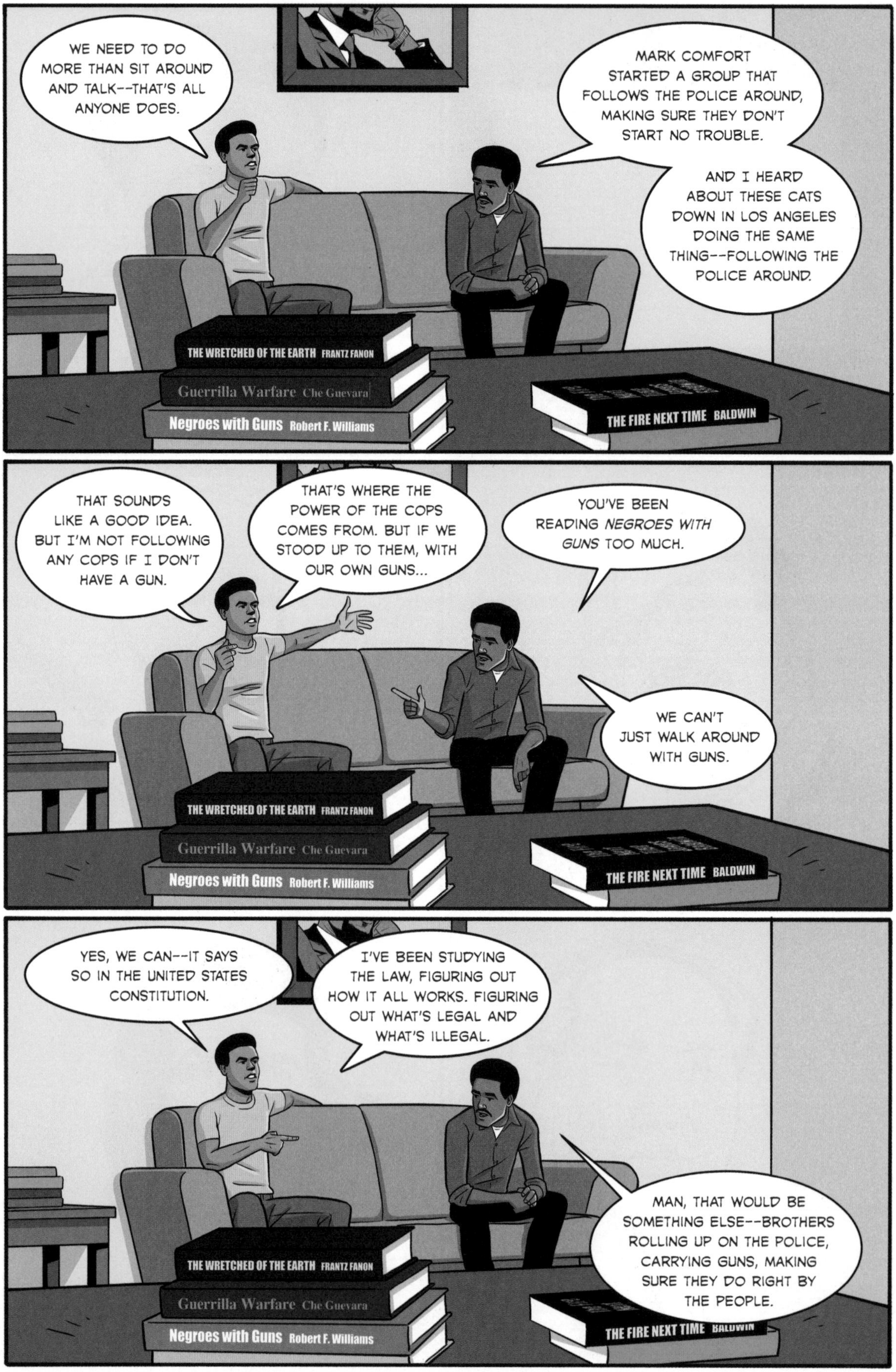
WE NEED TO DO MORE THAN SIT AROUND AND TALK--THAT'S ALL ANYONE DOES.
MARK COMFORT STARTED A GROUP THAT FOLLOWS THE POLICE AROUND, MAKING SURE THEY DON'T START NO TROUBLE.
AND I HEARD ABOUT THESE CATS DOWN IN LOS ANGELES DOING THE SAME THING--FOLLOWING THE POLICE AROUND.
THE WRETCHED OF THE EARTH FRANTZ FANON
Guerrilla Warfare Che Guevara
Negroes with Guns Robert F. Williams
THE FIRE NEXT TIME BALDWIN
THAT SOUNDS LIKE A GOOD IDEA. BUT I'M NOT FOLLOWING ANY COPS IF I DON'T HAVE A GUN.
THAT'S WHERE THE POWER OF THE COPS COMES FROM. BUT IF WE STOOD UP TO THEM, WITH OUR OWN GUNS...
YOU'VE BEEN READING *NEGROES WITH GUNS* TOO MUCH.
WE CAN'T JUST WALK AROUND WITH GUNS.
THE WRETCHED OF THE EARTH FRANTZ FANON
Guerrilla Warfare Che Guevara
Negroes with Guns Robert F. Williams
THE FIRE NEXT TIME BALDWIN
YES, WE CAN--IT SAYS SO IN THE UNITED STATES CONSTITUTION.
I'VE BEEN STUDYING THE LAW, FIGURING OUT HOW IT ALL WORKS. FIGURING OUT WHAT'S LEGAL AND WHAT'S ILLEGAL.
MAN, THAT WOULD BE SOMETHING ELSE--BROTHERS ROLLING UP ON THE POLICE, CARRYING GUNS, MAKING SURE THEY DO RIGHT BY THE PEOPLE.
THE WRETCHED OF THE EARTH FRANTZ FANON
Guerrilla Warfare Che Guevara
Negroes with Guns Robert F. Williams
THE FIRE NEXT TIME BALDWIN

ON SEPTEMBER 27, 1966, MATTHEW "PEANUT" JOHNSON WAS KILLED BY POLICE IN HUNTERS POINT, A POOR NEIGHBORHOOD IN EASTERN SAN FRANCISCO.

THE 16-YEAR-OLD JOHNSON WAS SHOT IN THE BACK, SETTING OFF THE HUNTERS POINT UPRISING.

BOTH THE CALIFORNIA HIGHWAY PATROL AND THE NATIONAL GUARD WERE DEPLOYED AS MARTIAL LAW WAS DECLARED BY GOVERNOR PAT BROWN. CIVIL UNREST LASTED FOR FIVE DAYS.

THE FOLLOWING MONTH, THE UC BERKELEY CHAPTER OF STUDENTS FOR A DEMOCRATIC SOCIETY HELD A CONFERENCE ON BLACK POWER. ONE OF THE MAIN SPEAKERS WAS STOKELY CARMICHAEL.

WE ARE OPPRESSED AS A GROUP BECAUSE WE ARE BLACK, NOT BECAUSE WE ARE LAZY, NOT BECAUSE WE'RE APATHETIC, NOT BECAUSE WE'RE STUPID, NOT BECAUSE WE SMELL, NOT BECAUSE WE EAT WATERMELON AND HAVE GOOD RHYTHM. WE ARE OPPRESSED BECAUSE WE ARE BLACK.

THE CONFERENCE AT BERKELEY BROUGHT INDIVIDUALS, ORGANIZATIONS, AND IDEAS AT THE FOREFRONT OF THE BLACK POWER MOVEMENT TO THE BAY AREA. THIS PROVED CRUCIAL FOR NEWTON AND SEALE, WHO WERE LOOKING FOR A WAY TO MAKE A DIFFERENCE.

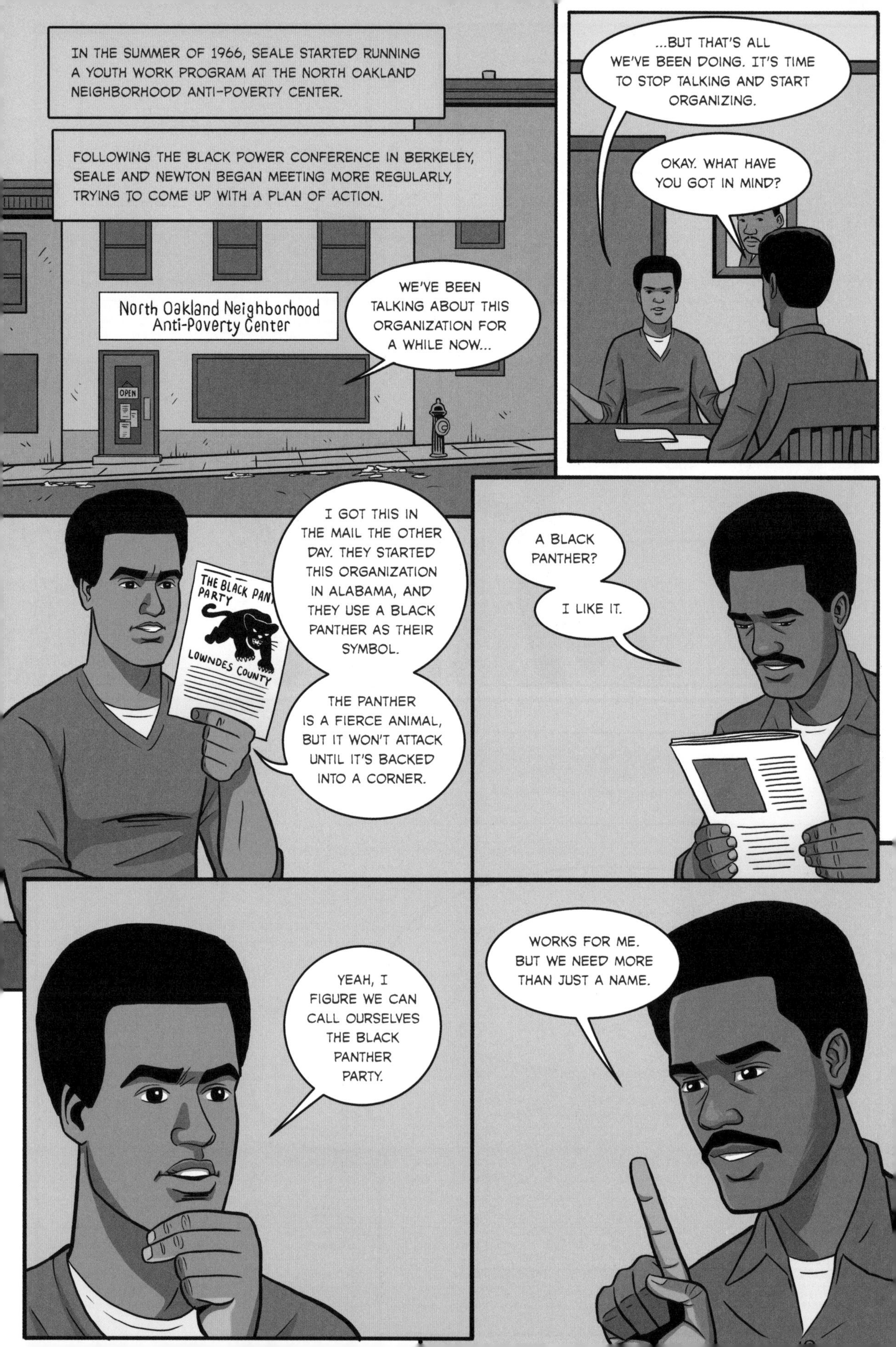
IN THE SUMMER OF 1966, SEALE STARTED RUNNING A YOUTH WORK PROGRAM AT THE NORTH OAKLAND NEIGHBORHOOD ANTI-POVERTY CENTER.
FOLLOWING THE BLACK POWER CONFERENCE IN BERKELEY, SEALE AND NEWTON BEGAN MEETING MORE REGULARLY, TRYING TO COME UP WITH A PLAN OF ACTION.
North Oakland Neighborhood Anti-Poverty Center
OPEN
WE'VE BEEN TALKING ABOUT THIS ORGANIZATION FOR A WHILE NOW...
...BUT THAT'S ALL WE'VE BEEN DOING. IT'S TIME TO STOP TALKING AND START ORGANIZING.
OKAY. WHAT HAVE YOU GOT IN MIND?
THE BLACK PAN PARTY
LOWNDES COUNTY
I GOT THIS IN THE MAIL THE OTHER DAY. THEY STARTED THIS ORGANIZATION IN ALABAMA, AND THEY USE A BLACK PANTHER AS THEIR SYMBOL.
THE PANTHER IS A FIERCE ANIMAL, BUT IT WON'T ATTACK UNTIL IT'S BACKED INTO A CORNER.
A BLACK PANTHER?
I LIKE IT.
YEAH, I FIGURE WE CAN CALL OURSELVES THE BLACK PANTHER PARTY.
WORKS FOR ME. BUT WE NEED MORE THAN JUST A NAME.

OVER THE COURSE OF SEVERAL DAYS IN OCTOBER 1966, WHILE WORKING OUT OF THE NORTH OAKLAND NEIGHBORHOOD ANTI-POVERTY CENTER, NEWTON AND SEALE DRAFTED THE TEN-POINT PROGRAM--THE GUIDING DOCUMENT FOR THE ORGANIZATION THEY WERE FORMING.

Ten Point Program: What We Want/What We Believe

1. We want freedom. We want power to determine the destiny of our Black community. We believe that Black people will not be free until we are able to determine our destiny.

2. We want full employment for our people. We believe that the federal government is responsible and obligated to give every man employment or a guaranteed income. We believe that if the White American business men will not give full employment, then the means of production should be taken from the business men and placed in the community so that the people of the community can organize and employ all of its people and give a high standard of living.

3. We want an end to the robbery by the White man of our Black community. We believe that this racist government has robbed us and now we are demanding the overdue debt of forty acres and two mules. Forty acres and two mules was promised 100 years ago as retribution for slave labor and mass murder of Black people. We will accept the payment in currency which will be distributed to our many communities: the Germans are now aiding the Jews in Israel for the genocide of the Jewish people. The Germans murdered 6,000,000 Jews. The American racist has taken part in the slaughter of over 50,000,000 Black people; therefore, we feel that this is a modest demand that we make.

4. We want decent housing, fit for shelter [of] human beings. We believe that if the White landlords will not give decent housing to our Black community, then the housing and the land should be made into cooperatives so that our community, with government aid, can build and make decent housing for its people.

5. We want education for our people that exposes the true nature of this decadent American society. We want education that teaches us our true history and our role in the present day society. We believe in an educational system that will give to our people a knowledge of self. If a man does not have knowledge of himself and his position in society and the world, then he has little chance to relate to anything else.

6. We want all Black men to be exempt from military service. We believe that Black people should not be forced to fight in the military service to defend a racist government that does not protect us. We will not fight and kill other people of color in the world who, like Black people, are being victimized by the White racist government of America. We will protect ourselves from the force and violence of the racist police and the racist military, by whatever means necessary.

7. We want an immediate end to *Police Brutality* and *Murder* of Black people. We believe we can end police brutality in our Black community by organizing Black *self defense* groups that are dedicated to defending our Black community from racist police oppression and brutality. The Second Amendment of the Constitution of the United States gives us the right to bear arms. We therefore believe that all Black people should arm themselves for *self defense*.

8. We want freedom for all Black men held in federal, state, county and city prisons and jails. We believe that all Black people should be released from the many jails and prisons because they have not received a fair and impartial trial.

9. We want all Black people when brought to trial to be tried in court by a jury of their peer group or people from their Black communities, as defined by the constitution of the United States. We believe that the courts should follow the United States Constitution so that Black people will receive fair trials. The 14th Amendment of the U.S. Constitution gives a man a right to be tried by his peers. A peer is a person from a similar economic, social, religious, geographical, environmental, historical and racial background. To do this the court will be forced to select a jury from the Black community from which the Black defendant came. We have been, and are being tried by all White juries that have no understanding of the "average reasoning man" of the Black community.

10. We want land, bread, housing, education, clothing, justice and peace. When in the course of human events, it becomes necessary for one people to dissolve the political bonds which have connected them with another, and to assume among the powers of the earth, the separate and equal station to which the laws of nature and nature's god entitle them, a decent respect to the opinions of mankind requires that they should declare the causes which impel them to separation. We hold these truths to be self-evident, that all men are created equal, that they are endowed by their creator with certain inalienable rights, that among these are life, liberty and the pursuit of happiness. That to secure these rights, governments are instituted among men, deriving their just powers from the consent of the governed, that *whenever any form of government becomes destructive of these ends, it is the right of people to alter or abolish it, and to institute new government, laying its foundation on such principles and organizing its power in such form as to them shall seem most likely to effect their safety and happiness.* Prudence, indeed, will dictate that governments long established should not be changed for light and transient causes; and accordingly all experience hath shewn, that mankind are more disposed to suffer, while evils are sufferable, than to right themselves by abolishing the forms to which they are accustomed. *But when a long train of abuses and usurpations, pursuing invariably the same object, evinces a design to reduce them under absolute despotism, it is their right, it is their duty, to throw off such government, and to provide new guards for their future security.*

ON OCTOBER 15, 1966, THE BLACK PANTHER PARTY FOR SELF-DEFENSE WAS OFFICIALLY BORN.

Lil' Bobby Hutton

BORN IN 1950, ROBERT JAMES HUTTON WAS THE FIRST MEMBER RECRUITED TO THE BLACK PANTHER PARTY. JUST 16 YEARS OLD AT THE TIME, HE WAS THE YOUNGEST OF THE FLEDGLING REVOLUTIONARIES.

HUTTON'S FAMILY HAD MOVED FROM ARKANSAS TO CALIFORNIA IN 1953, AFTER BEING HARASSED AND THREATENED BY THE KU KLUX KLAN.

A POOR STUDENT, HUTTON DROPPED OUT OF HIGH SCHOOL NOT KNOWING HOW TO READ. HE GOT A JOB AT THE NORTH OAKLAND NEIGHBORHOOD ANTI-POVERTY CENTER, WHERE HE BEFRIENDED SEALE, WHO TAUGHT HUTTON HOW TO READ.

SEALE TALKED TO HUTTON'S PARENTS TO GET PERMISSION FOR HIM TO JOIN THE BLACK PANTHERS. AFTER JOINING THE PARTY, SEALE AND NEWTON APPOINTED LIL' BOBBY AS NATIONAL TREASURER--EVEN THOUGH THE PANTHERS REALLY DIDN'T HAVE ANY MONEY.

TWO GUNS, HOWEVER, WERE NOT GOING TO BE ENOUGH.

THE FIRST GUNS CARRIED BY THE NEWLY FORMED BLACK PANTHER PARTY FOR SELF-DEFENSE CAME FROM SEALE'S PERSONAL COLLECTION.

RICHARD AOKI, A LOCAL RADICAL IN THE OAKLAND SCENE, DONATED GUNS TO THE PANTHERS. AOKI WAS AN ARMY VETERAN WHO SPENT PART OF HIS CHILD-HOOD IN A JAPANESE INTERNMENT CAMP.

AOKI WAS CLOSELY ASSOCIATED WITH THE PANTHERS IN THE GROUP'S EARLY DAYS. IN 2007, DOCUMENTS WERE UNCOVERED THAT IMPLICATED HIM AS AN INFORMANT FOR THE FBI.

AOKI DENIED THE CHARGES. TWO YEARS LATER, IN 2009, HE COMMITTED SUICIDE. SEVERAL YEARS LATER, MORE DOCUMENTS WERE DISCOVERED THAT DETAILED HIS WORK AS AN ALLEGED FBI INFORMANT.

ELBERT HOWARD.
BORN IN TENNESSEE.

BOBBY SEALE.
BORN IN TEXAS.

SHERWIN FORTE
(AKA SHERMAN).
BORN IN ALABAMA.

HUEY P. NEWTON.
BORN IN LOUISIANA.

REGINALD FORTE.
BORN IN ALABAMA.

BOBBY HUTTON.
BORN IN ARKANSAS.

LESS THAN A MONTH AFTER FORMING THE BLACK PANTHER PARTY FOR SELF-DEFENSE, SEALE AND NEWTON HAD RECRUITED THEIR FIRST FOUR MEMBERS. ALL SIX OF THE ORIGINAL MEMBERS WERE BORN IN THE SOUTH.

FIVE OF THE ORIGINAL SIX HAD RELOCATED TO CALIFORNIA AS PART OF THE GREAT MIGRATION WHEN THEY WERE CHILDREN; ELBERT "BIG MAN" HOWARD WAS THE ONLY ORIGINAL MEMBER TO COME TO CALIFORNIA FROM THE SOUTH AS AN ADULT.

THE ORIGINAL MEMBERS WERE FROM A YOUNGER GENERATION THAT WAS SUPPOSED TO HAVE IT BETTER THAN THEIR PARENTS AND GRANDPARENTS. UNFORTUNATELY, THEIR PREDECESSORS' BELIEF THAT A BETTER LIFE AWAITED IN NORTHERN CITIES HAD PROVEN FALSE. UNEMPLOYMENT, POVERTY, RACISM, AND POLICE BRUTALITY PLAGUED THE BLACK COMMUNITY IN THE NORTH AS WELL AS THE SOUTH.

UNLIKE THEIR PARENTS WHO HAD FLED THE SOUTH, THESE YOUNG MEN HAD NOWHERE ELSE TO GO. THEIR ONLY CHOICE WAS TO DEFEND THEMSELVES AGAINST THE SYSTEMS OF OPPRESSION.

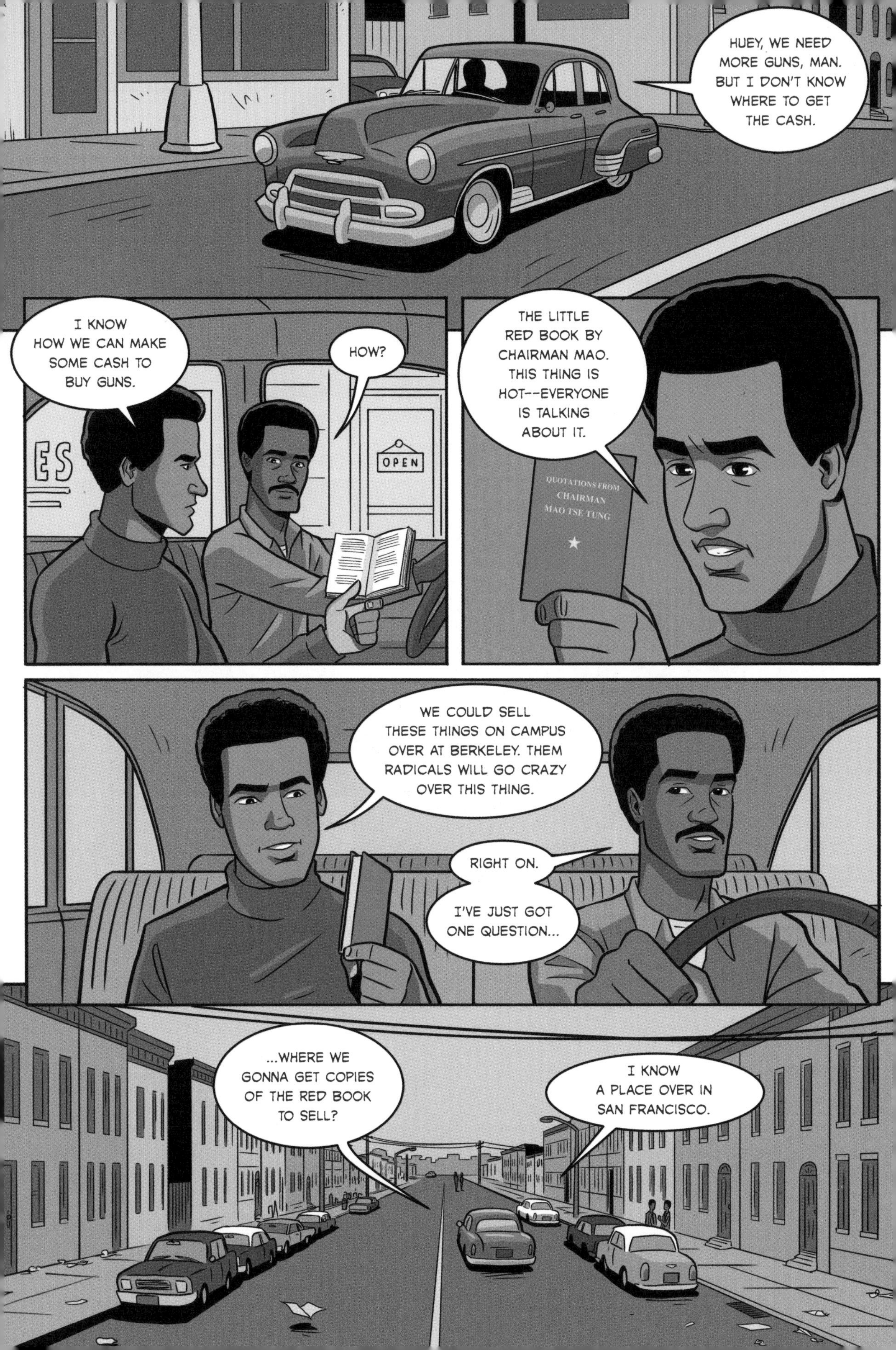
HUEY, WE NEED MORE GUNS, MAN. BUT I DON'T KNOW WHERE TO GET THE CASH.
I KNOW HOW WE CAN MAKE SOME CASH TO BUY GUNS.
HOW?
ES
OPEN
THE LITTLE RED BOOK BY CHAIRMAN MAO. THIS THING IS HOT--EVERYONE IS TALKING ABOUT IT.
QUOTATIONS FROM CHAIRMAN MAO TSE-TUNG
WE COULD SELL THESE THINGS ON CAMPUS OVER AT BERKELEY. THEM RADICALS WILL GO CRAZY OVER THIS THING.
RIGHT ON.
I'VE JUST GOT ONE QUESTION...
...WHERE WE GONNA GET COPIES OF THE RED BOOK TO SELL?
I KNOW A PLACE OVER IN SAN FRANCISCO.

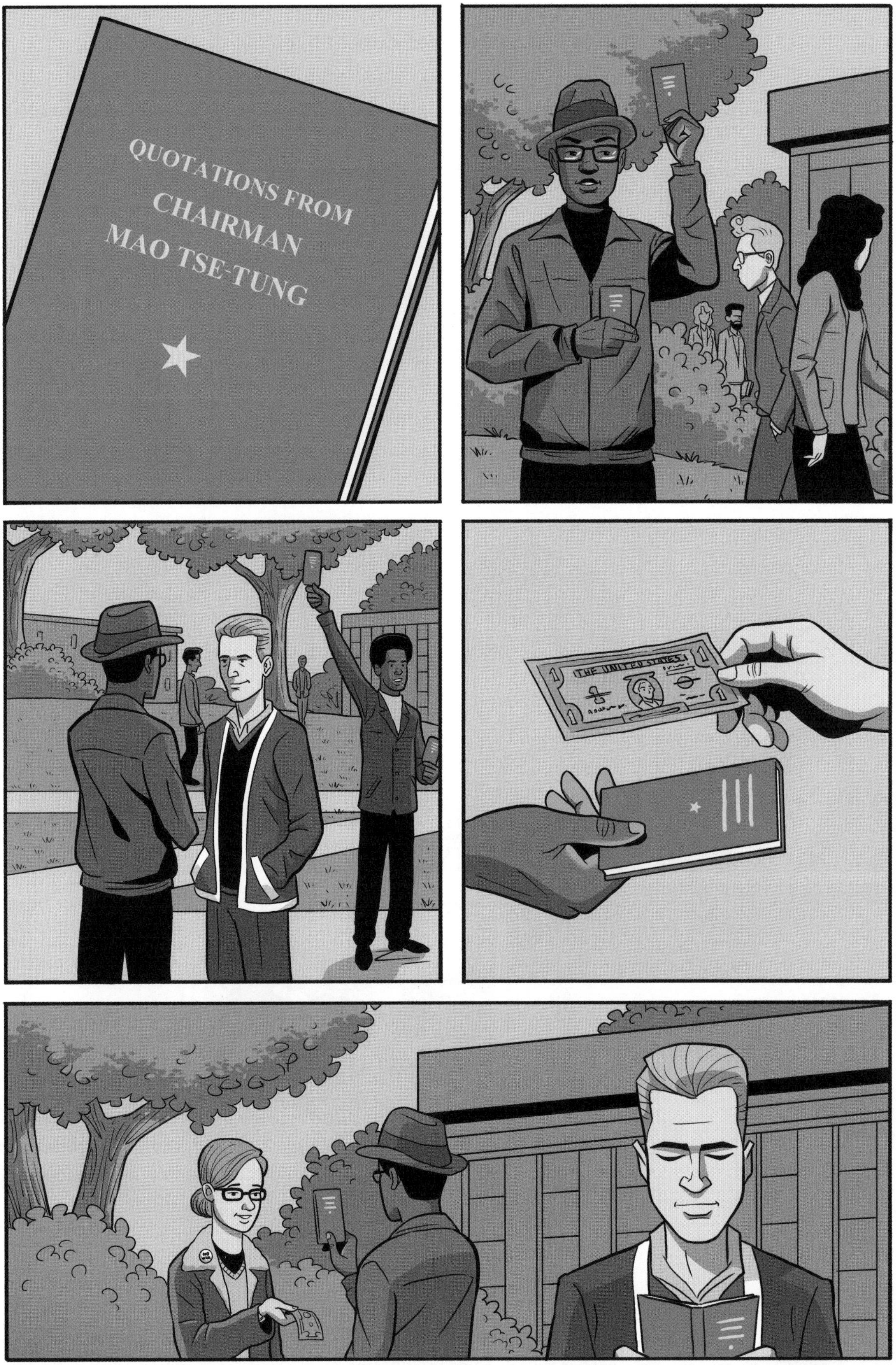
QUOTATIONS FROM
CHAIRMAN
MAO TSE-TUNG
THE UNITED STATES

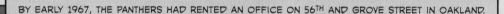

FOUR — 1967: PANTHERS UNLEASHED
AN EARLY ENCOUNTER*

BY EARLY 1967, THE PANTHERS HAD RENTED AN OFFICE ON 56TH AND GROVE STREET IN OAKLAND.

THEY WERE REGULARLY SEEN GOING IN AND OUT OF THEIR NEW HEADQUARTERS WITH GUNS. BUT, UP UNTIL THIS POINT, THEY HADN'T HAD ANY MAJOR CONFRONTATIONS WITH THE LAW.

ALL OF THAT WAS ABOUT TO CHANGE.

HERE COME THE PIGS.

GOOD.

THAT'S WHAT WE WANT.

JUST REMEMBER, WE AREN'T DOING ANYTHING WRONG.

WE AREN'T BREAKING ANY LAWS.

EVERYONE JUST KEEP COOL AND WAIT TO SEE WHAT THIS PIG DOES.

*INSPIRED BY TRUE EVENTS.

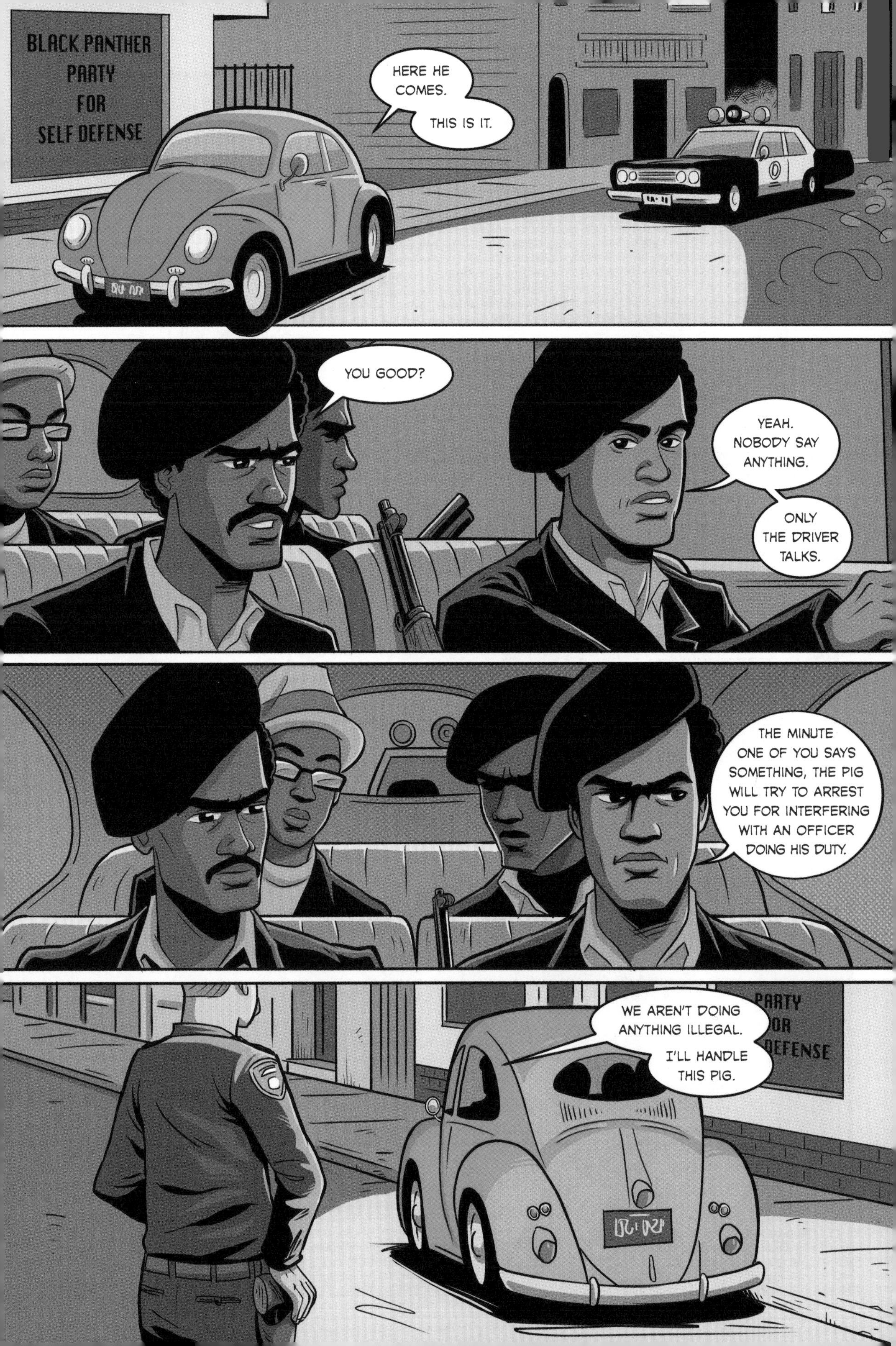
BLACK PANTHER PARTY FOR SELF DEFENSE
HERE HE COMES.
THIS IS IT.
YOU GOOD?
YEAH. NOBODY SAY ANYTHING.
ONLY THE DRIVER TALKS.
THE MINUTE ONE OF YOU SAYS SOMETHING, THE PIG WILL TRY TO ARREST YOU FOR INTERFERING WITH AN OFFICER DOING HIS DUTY.
WE AREN'T DOING ANYTHING ILLEGAL.
I'LL HANDLE THIS PIG.

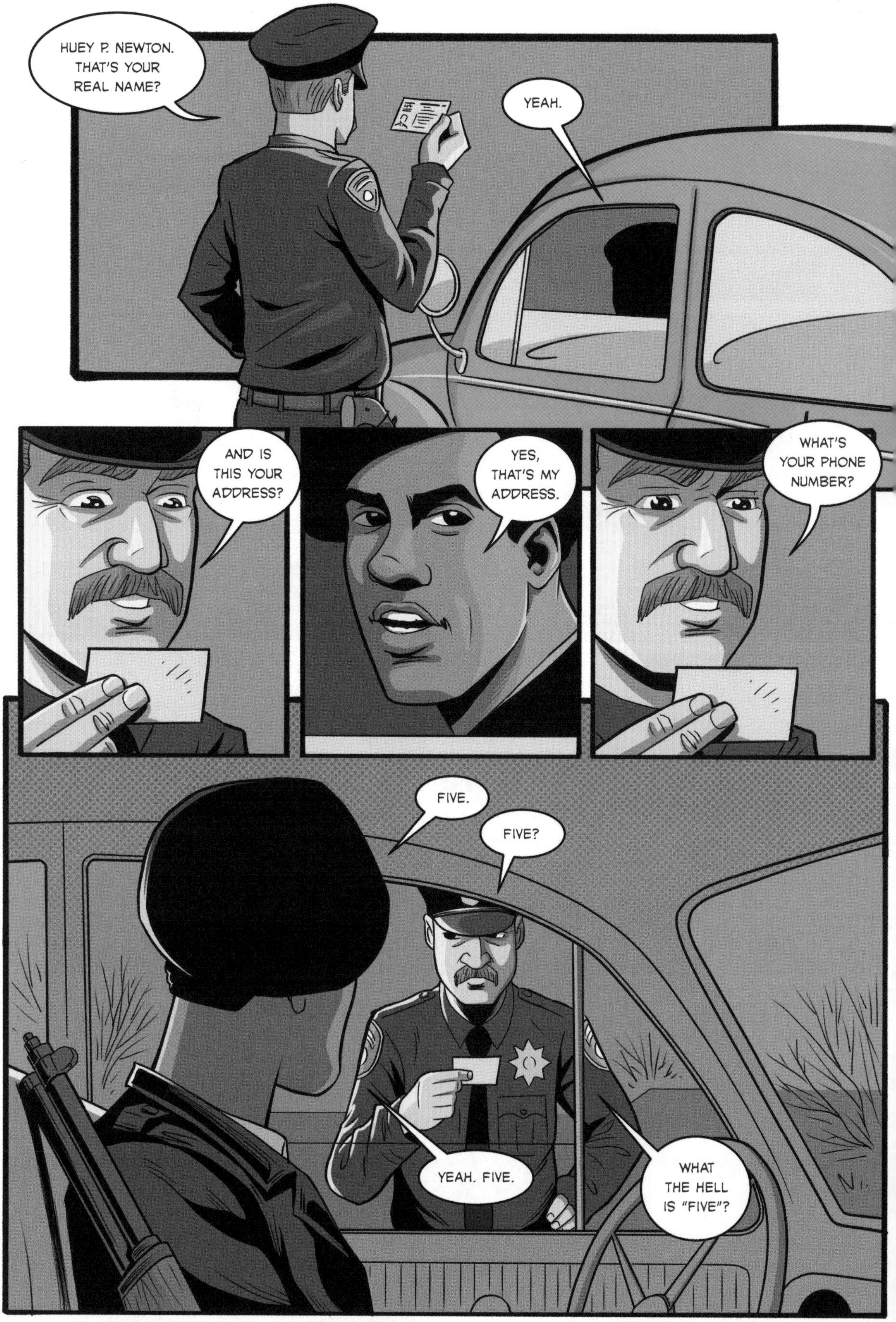
HUEY P. NEWTON. THAT'S YOUR REAL NAME?
YEAH.
AND IS THIS YOUR ADDRESS?
YES, THAT'S MY ADDRESS.
WHAT'S YOUR PHONE NUMBER?
FIVE.
FIVE?
YEAH. FIVE.
WHAT THE HELL IS "FIVE"?

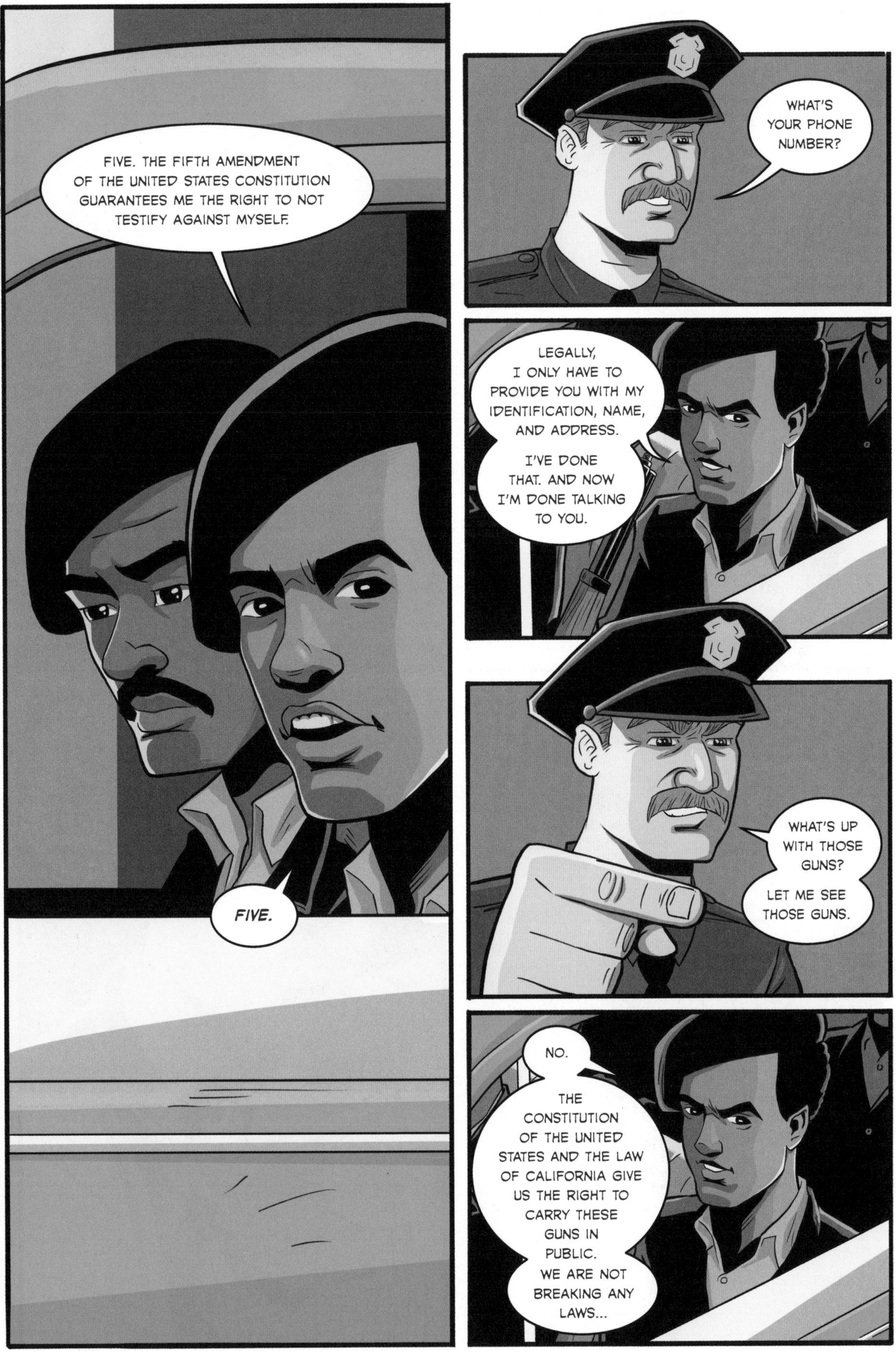
FIVE. THE FIFTH AMENDMENT OF THE UNITED STATES CONSTITUTION GUARANTEES ME THE RIGHT TO NOT TESTIFY AGAINST MYSELF.
FIVE.
WHAT'S YOUR PHONE NUMBER?
LEGALLY, I ONLY HAVE TO PROVIDE YOU WITH MY IDENTIFICATION, NAME, AND ADDRESS.
I'VE DONE THAT. AND NOW I'M DONE TALKING TO YOU.
WHAT'S UP WITH THOSE GUNS?
LET ME SEE THOSE GUNS.
NO.
THE CONSTITUTION OF THE UNITED STATES AND THE LAW OF CALIFORNIA GIVE US THE RIGHT TO CARRY THESE GUNS IN PUBLIC.
WE ARE NOT BREAKING ANY LAWS...

...AND YOU CAN'T SEE OUR GUNS.

I'M DONE TALKING TO YOU.

I ASKED YOU A QUESTION!

FIVE!

I WANT TO SEE THOSE GUNS.

WHO THE HELL DO YOU THINK YOU ARE?!

I SHOWED YOU MY IDENTIFICATION.

I'VE TOLD YOU EVERYTHING I'M REQUIRED TO TELL YOU BY LAW.

SO, THE QUESTION NOW IS THIS...

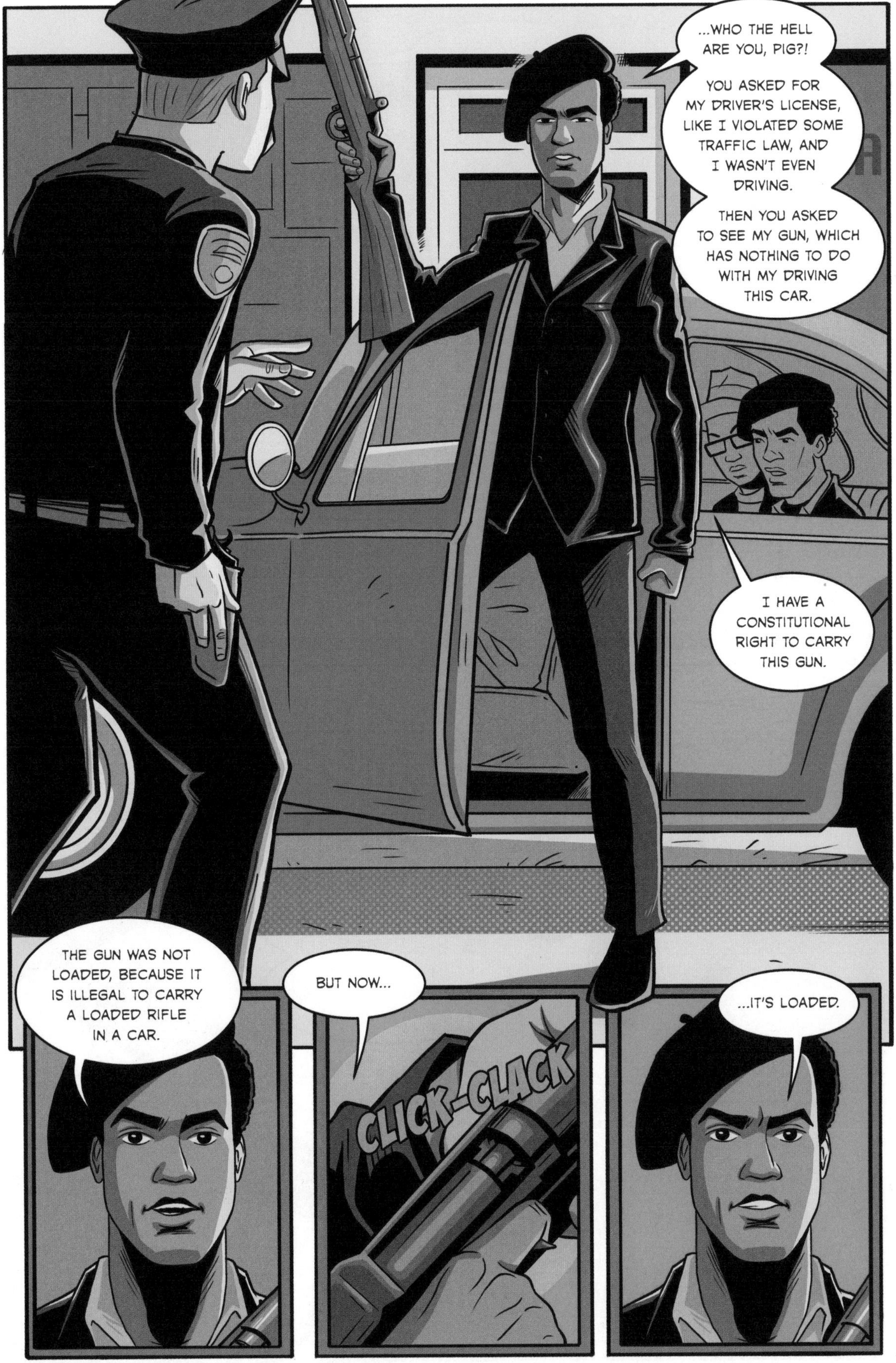

...WHO THE HELL ARE YOU, PIG?!
YOU ASKED FOR MY DRIVER'S LICENSE, LIKE I VIOLATED SOME TRAFFIC LAW, AND I WASN'T EVEN DRIVING.
THEN YOU ASKED TO SEE MY GUN, WHICH HAS NOTHING TO DO WITH MY DRIVING THIS CAR.
I HAVE A CONSTITUTIONAL RIGHT TO CARRY THIS GUN.
THE GUN WAS NOT LOADED, BECAUSE IT IS ILLEGAL TO CARRY A LOADED RIFLE IN A CAR.
BUT NOW...
CLICK-CLACK
...IT'S LOADED.

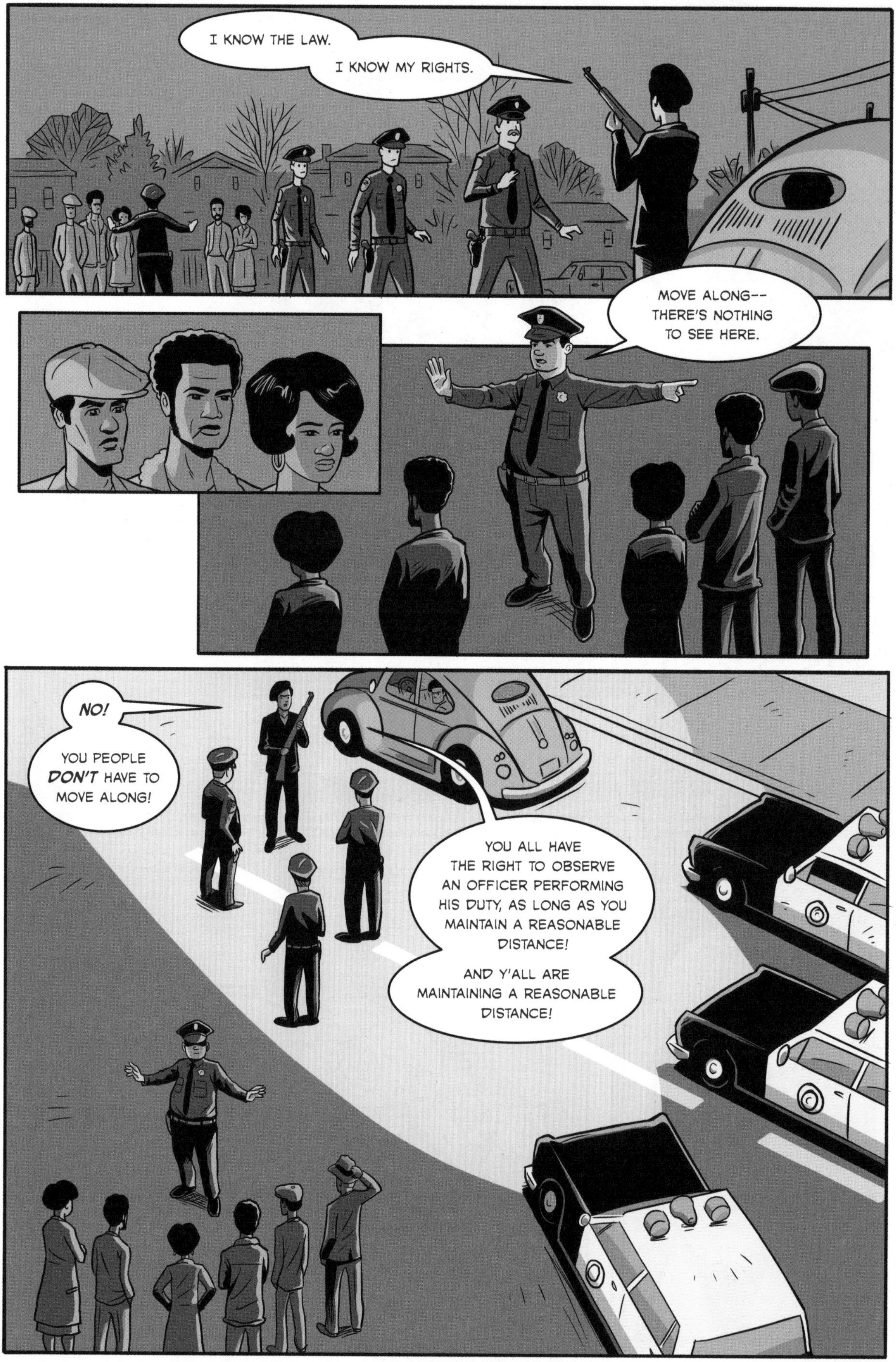
I KNOW THE LAW.
I KNOW MY RIGHTS.
MOVE ALONG-- THERE'S NOTHING TO SEE HERE.
NO!
YOU PEOPLE ***DON'T*** HAVE TO MOVE ALONG!
YOU ALL HAVE THE RIGHT TO OBSERVE AN OFFICER PERFORMING HIS DUTY, AS LONG AS YOU MAINTAIN A REASONABLE DISTANCE!
AND Y'ALL ARE MAINTAINING A REASONABLE DISTANCE!

YOU DON'T HAVE TO GO ANYWHERE.

WHAT'RE YOU DOING WITH THAT GUN?

I'M DEFENDING MYSELF, WHICH IS MY LEGAL RIGHT.

AND I'M WARNING YOU, IF YOU REACH FOR YOUR GUN--IF *ANY* OF YOU PIGS REACH FOR YOUR GUNS...

...I'LL BLOW YOUR BRAINS OUT.

YOU HEAR ME, YOU RACIST PIGS?

THE *BLACK PANTHER PARTY FOR SELF-DEFENSE* IS HERE TO PROTECT OURSELVES AND OUR COMMUNITY FROM THE VIOLENT, RACIST ATTACKS OF FASCIST PIGS LIKE *YOU*.

THAT'S WHAT I'M DOING WITH MY GUN. WHAT'RE YOU GONNA DO WITH *YOUR* GUNS?

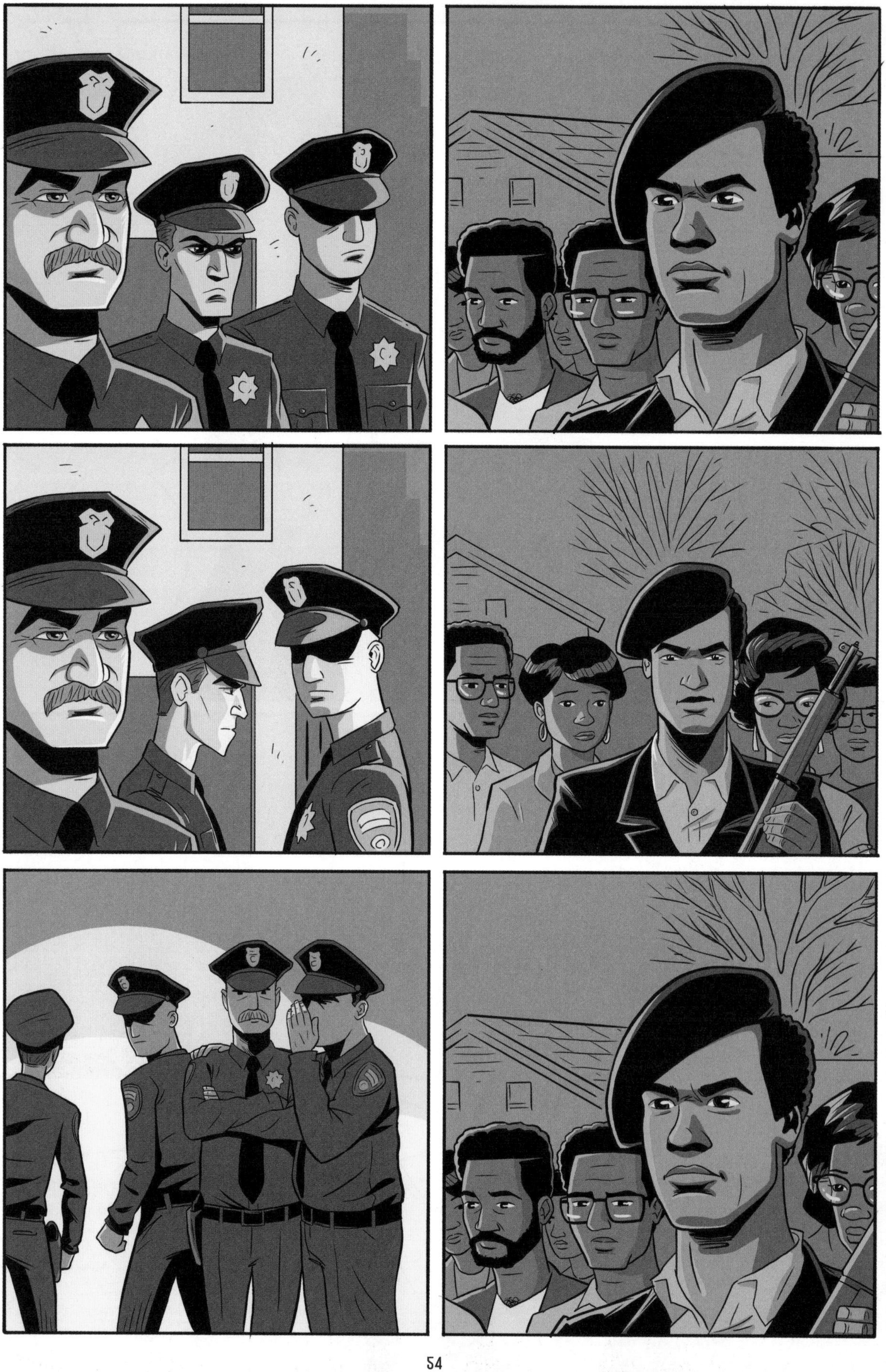

IN FEBRUARY 1967, LESS THAN SIX MONTHS AFTER FORMING, THE **BLACK PANTHER PARTY FOR SELF-DEFENSE** HAD THEIR FIRST ENCOUNTER WITH THE POLICE IN OAKLAND.

NOT A SINGLE SHOT WAS FIRED, AND NO ONE WAS INJURED.

BUT WAR HAD BEEN DECLARED.

THE INTERSECTION AT 55TH STREET AND MARKET STREET IN OAKLAND WAS AN EXCEPTIONALLY BUSY THOROUGHFARE WITH NO TRAFFIC LIGHT.

IT WAS A DANGEROUS INTERSECTION, WITH FREQUENT ACCIDENTS. SEVERAL BLACK CHILDREN FROM A NEARBY SCHOOL HAD BEEN HIT BY PASSING CARS, WITH AT LEAST ONE FATALITY.

MEMBERS OF THE COMMUNITY REACHED OUT TO THE BLACK PANTHERS FOR HELP IN TRYING TO GET THE CITY TO INSTALL A TRAFFIC LIGHT, BUT THE CITY CLAIMED THERE WAS NO BUDGET FOR IT.

DETERMINED TO KEEP THE NEIGHBORHOOD SAFE AND SERVE THE COMMUNITY, THE PANTHERS BEGAN TO SERVE AS CROSSING GUARDS BOTH BEFORE AND AFTER SCHOOL.

STOP

WITHIN SEVERAL MONTHS, THE CITY INSTALLED A TRAFFIC LIGHT, DESPITE ITS EARLIER CLAIMS OF NOT HAVING THE BUDGET.

Eldridge Cleaver

ELDRIDGE CLEAVER
WAS BORN IN 1935 IN
ARKANSAS AND MOVED
WITH HIS FAMILY TO LOS
ANGELES DURING WWII.
AFTER SEVERAL RUN-INS
WITH THE LAW, CLEAVER
WAS SENTENCED TO TWO
AND A HALF YEARS IN
PRISON FOR POSSESSION
OF MARIJUANA IN 1954. HE
WAS JUST 19 YEARS OLD.

WHILE INCARCERATED AT
SOLEDAD STATE PRISON,
CLEAVER EARNED HIS HIGH
SCHOOL DIPLOMA WHILE
STUDYING A WIDE RANGE
OF WORKS BY WRITERS
SUCH AS W. E. B. DU BOIS,
KARL MARX, AND MACHIAVELLI.

WITHIN A YEAR OF BEING RELEASED FROM PRISON IN 1957, CLEAVER WAS ONCE AGAIN INCARCERATED AND SENTENCED TO 14 YEARS FOR ASSAULT WITH INTENT TO KILL. IN FOLSOM STATE PRISON, HE BECAME POLITICIZED, JOINED THE NATION OF ISLAM, AND CLAIMED TO HAVE FALLEN IN LOVE WITH BEVERLY AXELROD, A WHITE CIVIL RIGHTS ATTORNEY.

DURING HIS TIME AT FOLSOM, CLEAVER BEGAN WRITING ESSAYS AND LETTERS—INCLUDING LOVE LETTERS TO AXELROD—THAT DESCRIBED HIS LIFE AS A CRIMINAL AND SERIAL RAPIST, AND HIS TRANSFORMATION INTO A POLITICAL THINKER.

WITH THE HELP OF AXELROD, CLEAVER'S WRITING BEGAN TO APPEAR IN *RAMPARTS* MAGAZINE, AND IT HELPED GARNER HIM A FOLLOWING, ESPECIALLY AMONG BLACK POLITICAL ACTIVISTS. PAROLED IN 1966, HE MOVED TO SAN FRANCISCO AND WENT TO WORK FOR *RAMPARTS*. TWO YEARS LATER, HIS COLLECTED WRITING WAS PUBLISHED AS *SOUL ON ICE*.

THROUGH HIS WORK AT *RAMPARTS* AND HIS POLITICAL ACTIVITY, CLEAVER BECAME SOMETHING OF A CELEBRITY IN THE BAY AREA. HE COFOUNDED BLACK HOUSE, A CULTURAL CENTER DESIGNED TO FOSTER THE GROWING BLACK POWER MOVEMENT.

IT WAS AT THIS TIME THAT HE FIRST MET NEWTON AND SEALE, WHO INVITED HIM TO JOIN THE BLACK PANTHER PARTY FOR SELF-DEFENSE. BUT CLEAVER DECLINED, BECAUSE HE WAS ALREADY A MEMBER OF ANOTHER BLACK PANTHER PARTY.

The Other Black Panthers

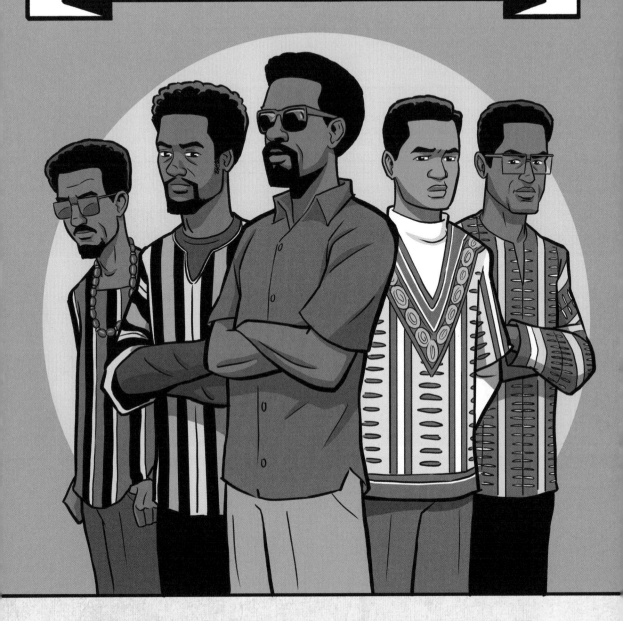

THE EARLY HISTORY OF THE BLACK PANTHER PARTY FOR SELF-DEFENSE CAN GET CONFUSING, AS THERE WERE MULTIPLE GROUPS CALLING THEMSELVES THE BLACK PANTHERS. THE ORIGINAL BLACK PANTHER PARTY WAS THE NICKNAME GIVEN TO THE LOWNDES COUNTY FREEDOM ORGANIZATION (LCFO).

WITH THE GROWTH OF THE BLACK POWER MOVEMENT, ORGANIZATIONS INSPIRED BY THE LCFO'S POLITICAL PARTY BEGAN TO DEVELOP. IN CITIES LIKE LOS ANGELES AND CHICAGO, GROUPS WITH NAMES LIKE "THE BLACK PANTHER POLITICAL PARTY" BEGAN TO APPEAR.

IN SAN FRANCISCO, THE BLACK PANTHER PARTY OF NORTHERN CALIFORNIA GREW OUT OF REVOLUTIONARY ACTION MOVEMENT (RAM). CLEAVER JOINED UP WITH THE RAM-AFFILIATED GROUP OF PANTHERS WHEN HE MOVED TO SAN FRANCISCO.

THESE OTHER ORGANIZATIONS WOULD EVENTUALLY DISBAND BY 1969, LEAVING ONLY THE OAKLAND-BASED BLACK PANTHER PARTY FOR SELF-DEFENSE, WHICH SHORTENED ITS NAME TO THE BLACK PANTHER PARTY IN 1968.

GUARDING SISTER BETTY

FEBRUARY 21, 1967

HAVING MADE A NAME FOR THEMSELVES IN OAKLAND, THE BLACK PANTHER PARTY FOR SELF-DEFENSE WAS ASKED BY ELDRIDGE CLEAVER AND THE RAM-AFFILIATED BLACK PANTHER PARTY OF NORTHERN CALIFORNIA TO HELP PROVIDE SECURITY FOR BETTY SHABAZZ, THE WIDOW OF MALCOLM X.

SHABAZZ WAS IN SAN FRANCISCO TO SPEAK AT A CONFERENCE. NEWTON, SEALE, AND A GROUP OF ARMED PANTHERS MET HER AT THE AIRPORT, WHERE THEY IMMEDIATELY CAUGHT THE ATTENTION OF BOTH AIRPORT SECURITY AND THE POLICE.

DESPITE AN EXCHANGE OF WORDS, THERE WAS NO MAJOR INCIDENT BETWEEN THE PANTHERS AND AIRPORT AUTHORITIES. THE PANTHERS ESCORTED SHABAZZ TO THE OFFICES OF *RAMPARTS* MAGAZINE. THIS IS WHERE THE REAL TROUBLE BEGAN.

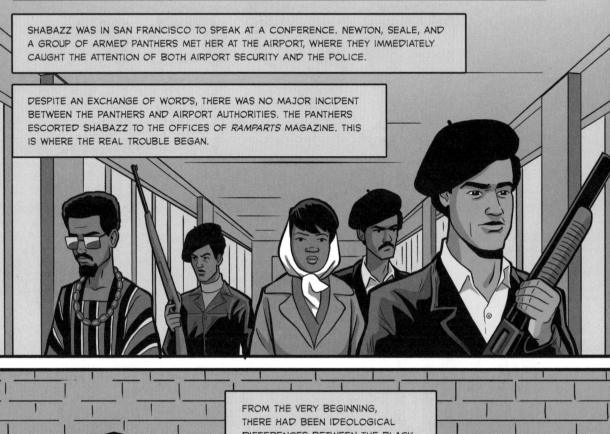

FROM THE VERY BEGINNING, THERE HAD BEEN IDEOLOGICAL DIFFERENCES BETWEEN THE BLACK PANTHER PARTY FOR SELF-DEFENSE AND THE BLACK PANTHER PARTY OF NORTHERN CALIFORNIA.

SEALE CALLED THE SAN FRANCISCO GROUP THE "PAPER PANTHERS," BECAUSE THEY WERE HESITANT TO TAKE UP ARMS AND CONFRONT THE POLICE.

WHILE LEAVING THE OFFICES OF *RAMPARTS*, SHABAZZ MADE A REQUEST OF THE PANTHERS.

PLEASE, I DON'T WANT ANYONE TAKING PICTURES.

ANYTHING YOU SAY, SISTER SHABAZZ.

NO PICTURES.

CLICK CLICK CLICK

I SAID, NO PICTURES!

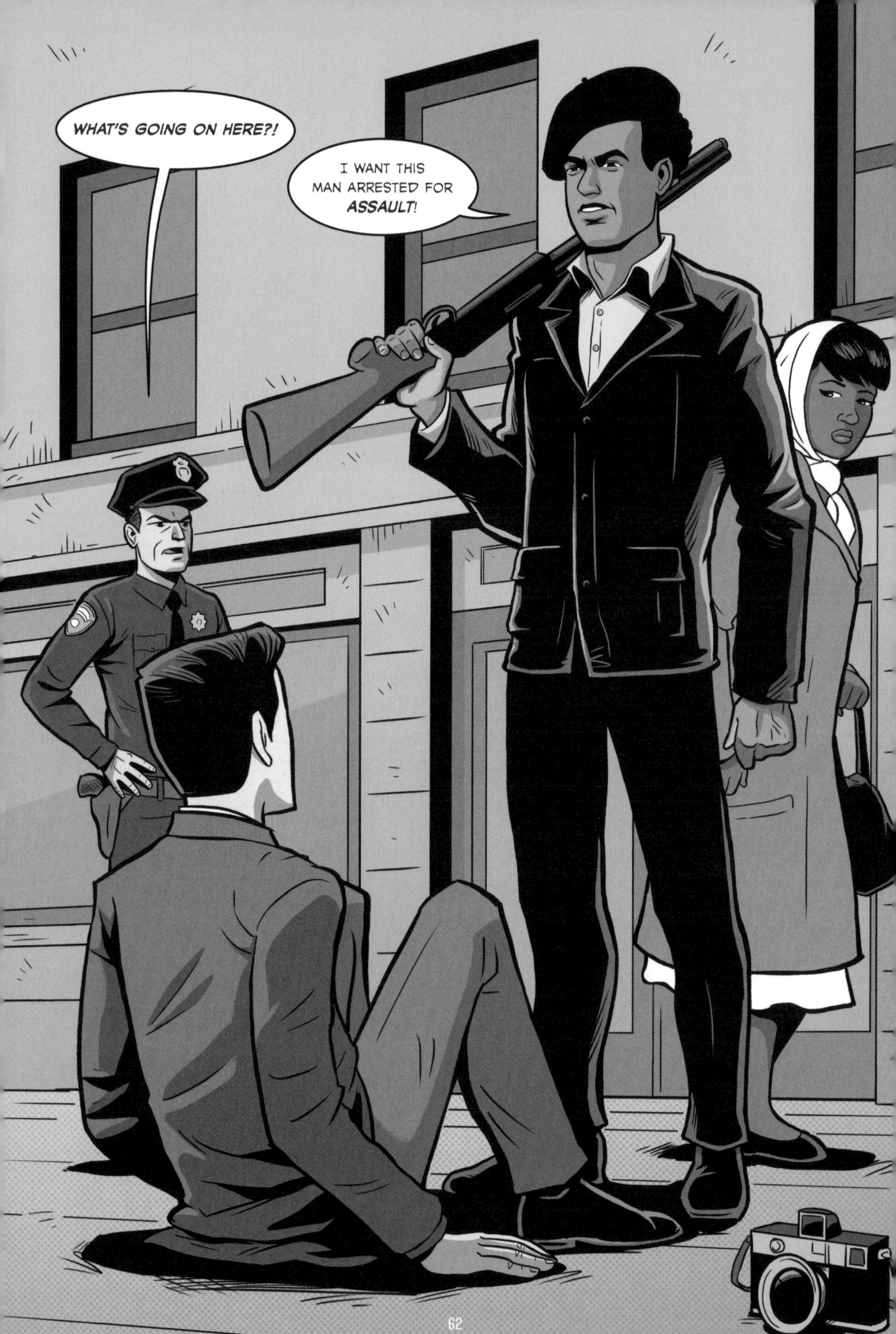
WHAT'S GOING ON HERE?!
I WANT THIS MAN ARRESTED FOR ASSAULT!

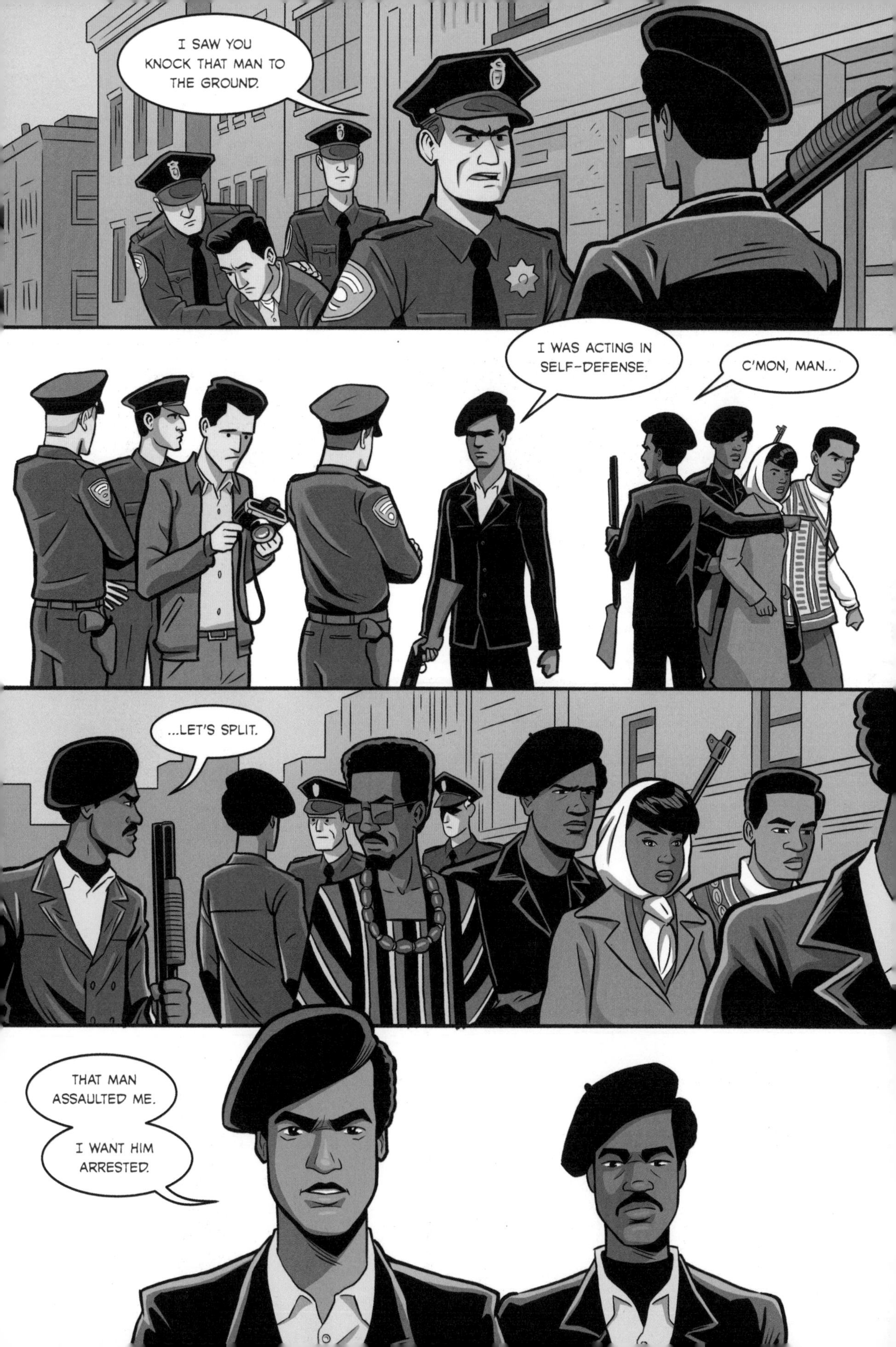
I SAW YOU KNOCK THAT MAN TO THE GROUND.
I WAS ACTING IN SELF-DEFENSE.
C'MON, MAN...
...LET'S SPLIT.
THAT MAN ASSAULTED ME.
I WANT HIM ARRESTED.

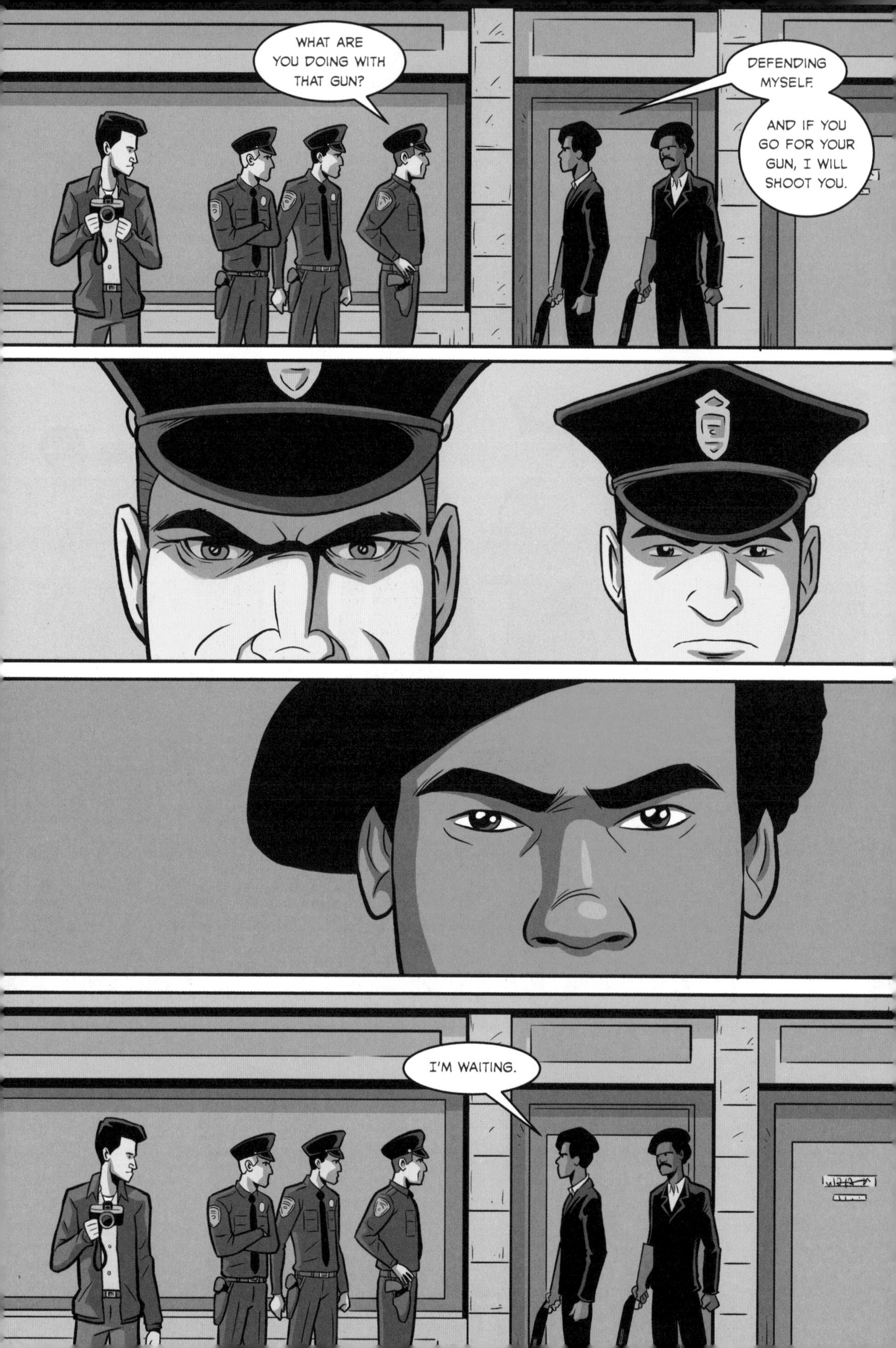
WHAT ARE YOU DOING WITH THAT GUN?
DEFENDING MYSELF.
AND IF YOU GO FOR YOUR GUN, I WILL SHOOT YOU.
I'M WAITING.

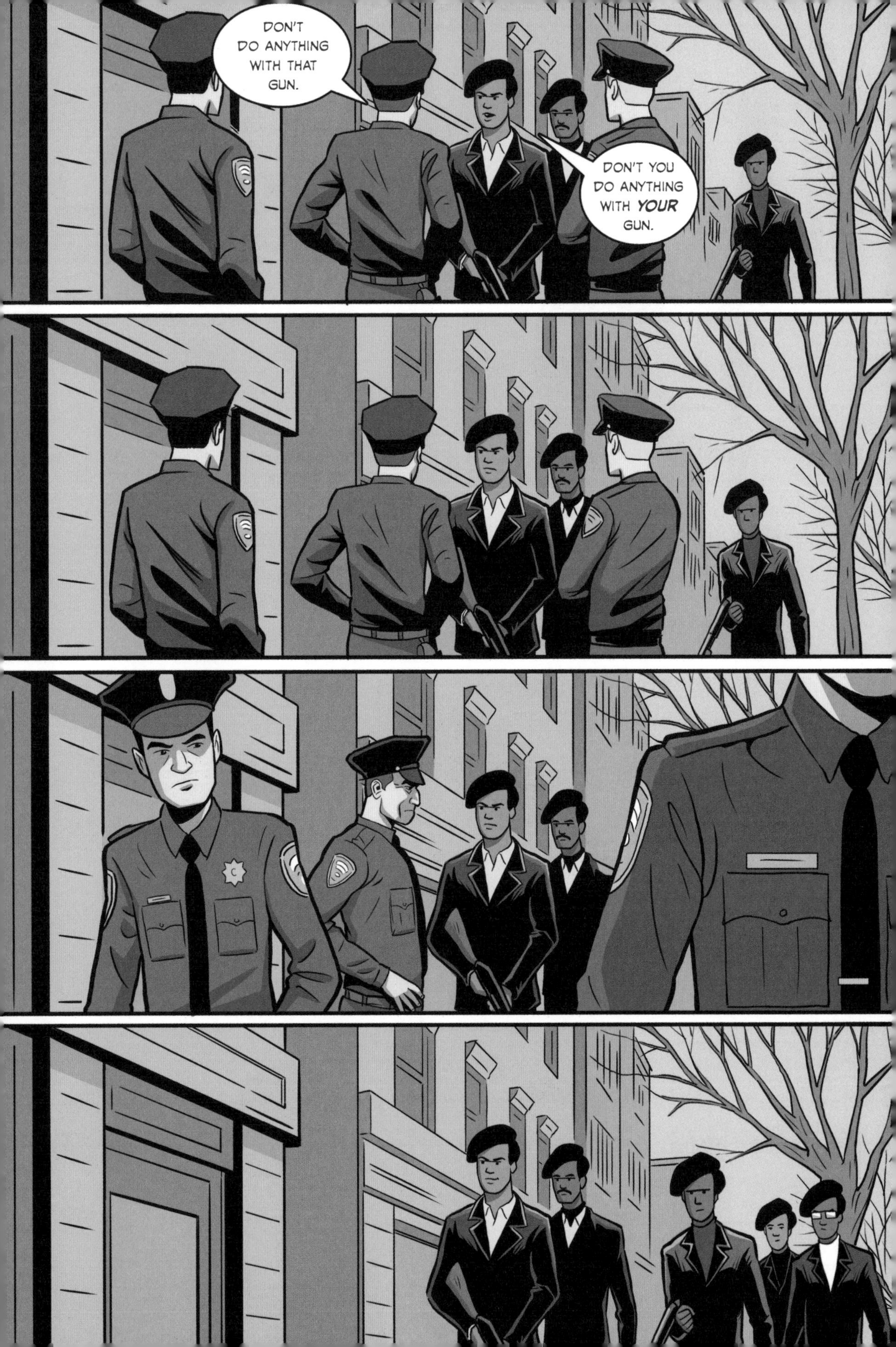
DON'T DO ANYTHING WITH THAT GUN.
DON'T YOU DO ANYTHING WITH YOUR GUN.

NEWTON AND SEALE HAD ASKED CLEAVER TO JOIN THE BLACK PANTHER PARTY FOR SELF-DEFENSE.

AT FIRST, CLEAVER DECLINED THEIR INVITATION.

BUT AFTER WITNESSING NEWTON STAND UP TO THE POLICE AFTER PROTECTING BETTY SHABAZZ ON FEBRUARY 21, 1967, CLEAVER CHANGED HIS MIND.

THE MURDER OF DENZIL DOWELL

ON APRIL 1, 1967, IN RICHMOND, A CITY NORTH OF OAKLAND, 22-YEAR-OLD DENZIL DOWELL WAS KILLED BY POLICE. DOWELL WAS ONE OF SEVERAL YOUNG BLACK PEOPLE TO BE KILLED BY POLICE IN AND AROUND RICHMOND.

DOWELL'S FAMILY DID NOT BELIEVE THE POLICE REPORTS OF HIS DEATH, BUT THEIR QUESTIONS WENT UNANSWERED. WITH NO ONE TO TURN TO, MARK COMFORT INTRODUCED THE DOWELL FAMILY TO THE NEWLY FORMED BLACK PANTHER PARTY FOR SELF-DEFENSE.

THE PANTHERS BEGAN THEIR OWN INVESTIGATION OF THE KILLING OF DOWELL, EXAMINING THE CRIME SCENE AND TALKING TO MEMBERS OF THE COMMUNITY WHO HAD HEARD THE SHOOTING. THEY QUICKLY UNCOVERED SEVERAL INCONSISTENCIES IN THE POLICE REPORT.

THE POLICE CLAIMED THAT DOWELL WAS SHOT THREE TIMES, AND THAT HE HAD BEEN RUNNING AWAY FROM THE SCENE OF A CRIME.

IN FACT, DOWELL HAD BEEN SHOT SIX TIMES, AND HIS WOUNDS PROVED THAT HE HAD BEEN FACING HIS KILLERS, WITH HIS HANDS RAISED ABOVE HIS HEAD.

OTHER FACTS FROM THE POLICE REPORT DID NOT LINE UP WITH FORENSIC OR CRIME-SCENE EVIDENCE. FOR EXAMPLE, THERE WAS NO BLOOD ON THE GROUND NEAR DOWELL'S BODY, INDICATING IT HAD BEEN MOVED AFTER HE WAS SHOT.

THE MORE LIKELY SCENARIO WAS THAT DOWELL HAD BEEN KILLED BY A COUNTY SHERIFF'S DEPUTY WITH A HISTORY OF RACISM AND A PERSONAL GRUDGE AGAINST HIM.

IN THE WEEKS FOLLOWING THE KILLING OF DENZIL DOWELL, SEVERAL RALLIES WERE HELD BY THE PANTHERS IN RICHMOND IN AN EFFORT TO BRING ATTENTION TO THE BRUTALITY OF LAW ENFORCEMENT.

TO HELP PUBLICIZE THE RALLY, THE PANTHERS DISTRIBUTED THE FIRST ISSUE OF *THE BLACK PANTHER*.

THE FIRST ISSUE OF THE NEWSPAPER WAS NOTHING MORE THAN A NEWSLETTER—TWO PAGES STAPLED TOGETHER WITH INFORMATION ABOUT THE KILLING OF DENZIL DOWELL AND AN UPCOMING RALLY.

The BLACK PANTHER

NEWS SERVICE NUMBER 1

VOLUME 1   APRIL 25, 1967
P.O. BOX 8641 OAK. CALIF EMERYVILLE BRANCH

PUBLISHED BY THE BLACK PANTHER PARTY FOR SELF DEFENSE

WHY WAS DENZIL DOWELL KILLED

APRIL FIRST 3:50 aM

"I BELIEVE THE POLICE MURDERED MY SON" SAYS THE MOTHER OF DENZIL DOWELL.

THREE THOUSAND COPIES OF *THE BLACK PANTHER* NEWSLETTER WERE HANDED OUT. FOR THE FIRST TIME SINCE THE FOUNDING OF THE ORGANIZATION, THE PANTHERS FULLY CONNECTED WITH THE COMMUNITY.

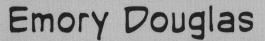

Emory Douglas

EMORY DOUGLAS WAS AMONG THE EARLIEST MEMBERS TO JOIN THE BLACK PANTHERS IN 1967, AND HE WAS ALREADY ASSOCIATED WITH THE RAM-AFFILIATED BLACK PANTHER PARTY OF NORTHERN CALIFORNIA.

DOUGLAS FIRST MET NEWTON AND SEALE WHEN THE OAKLAND-BASED PANTHERS WORKED WITH THE SAN FRANCISCO-BASED GROUP TO PROVIDE SECURITY FOR BETTY SHABAZZ.

LEAVING ONE BLACK PANTHER PARTY FOR ANOTHER, DOUGLAS BEGAN USING HIS ARTISTIC SKILLS WHILE WORKING ON THE NEWLY FORMED *BLACK PANTHER* NEWSPAPER. EVERY WEEK, HIS STYLISH AND DISTINCTIVE ILLUSTRATIONS APPEARED IN *THE BLACK PANTHER*, DEFINING THE VISUAL IDENTITY OF BOTH THE NEWSPAPER AND THE PARTY.

IF *THE BLACK PANTHER* WAS THE MOST IMPORTANT WAY THE PANTHERS COMMUNICATED WITH THE WORLD (AND AMONG CHAPTERS), THEN THE ART OF EMORY DOUGLAS WAS AN INVALUABLE TOOL IN HOW THE NEWSPAPER CAPTURED THE IMAGINATION OF THE PUBLIC AND CONVEYED THE IDEAS EXPRESSED WITHIN ITS PAGES.

LESS THAN A MONTH AFTER THE FIRST EDITION WAS PUBLISHED, *THE BLACK PANTHER* EVOLVED FROM A NEWSLETTER TO A WEEKLY NEWSPAPER, AND IT BECAME A CORNERSTONE OF THE ORGANIZATION AS IT BEGAN TO GROW. IN AN ERA BEFORE THE INTERNET, THE NEWSPAPER ALLOWED DIFFERENT CHAPTERS TO COMMUNICATE WHAT WAS HAPPENING IN THEIR PART OF THE COUNTRY.

THE BLACK PANTHER
INTERCOMMUNAL NEWS SERVICE   25 cents
VOL VI NO 7   Copyright © 1971 by Huey P. Newton   SATURDAY, MARCH 13, 1971
THE BLACK PANTHER PARTY

FREE ANGELA

THE BLACK PANTHER   25 cents
Black Community News Service
SATURDAY, DECEMBER 6, 1969
THE BLACK PANTHER PARTY

"THE ISSUE IS THE POLITICAL PRISONERS OF AMERICA. AND PEOPLE AS ONE TO STAND FOR THE RELEASE OF ALL POLITICAL PRISONERS."

HUEY P. NEWTON,
MINISTER OF DEFENSE

PUBLISHED FROM 1967 TO 1980, THERE WERE 537 ISSUES OF *THE BLACK PANTHER*, WITH CIRCULATION REACHING 300,000. *THE BLACK PANTHER* WAS NOT ONLY ONE OF THE MOST IMPORTANT ENDEAVORS OF THE PARTY, IT WAS ALSO ITS MOST ENDURING.

INSIDE THIS ISSUE..
Huey P. Newton to the R.N.A.
Article from Comrade Kim Il Sung from the D.P.R.K.

THE PAPER WAS PRINTED ON WEDNESDAYS, PICKED UP ON THURSDAYS, AND SHIPPED TO VARIOUS CHAPTERS AND BRANCHES ALL OVER THE COUNTRY ON FRIDAYS. FROM THERE, IT WAS SOLD IN STORES AND ON STREET CORNERS, OFTEN BY YOUNG PEOPLE.

THE NEWSPAPER BECAME A PRIMARY SOURCE OF INCOME FOR BOTH THE PARTY AND ITS MEMBERS. PROCEEDS WERE SPLIT BETWEEN THE NATIONAL OFFICE, THE LOCAL CHAPTER, AND WHOEVER SOLD THE PAPER.

PART OF THE REVENUE WAS USED TO COVER THE EXPENSE OF MAINTAINING "PANTHER PADS," WHICH WERE COMMUNAL LIVING SPACES THAT HOUSED PARTY MEMBERS. FOR MANY MEMBERS OF THE PARTY, SELLING THE PAPER WAS THEIR MAIN SOURCE OF INCOME.

THE BLACK PANTHER 25 CENTS

THE BLACK PANTHER PARTY

BLACK LIBERATION STRUGGLE SHOWS PROGRESS

THE SACRAMENTO INCIDENT

WITH THE ACTIVITIES OF THE PANTHERS GETTING MORE PRESS, THEIR ACTIONS CAUGHT THE ATTENTION LAW ENFORCEMENT AND POLITICIANS, INCLUDING CALIFORNIA STATE ASSEMBLYMAN DON MULFORD.

SIX WEEKS AFTER THE PANTHERS PROVIDED SECURITY FOR BETTY SHABAZZ AND CLASHED WITH POLICE, MULFORD INTRODUCED BILL AB-1591 IN THE LEGISLATURE ON APRIL 5, 1967.

THE BILL WOULD MAKE IT ILLEGAL TO CARRY LOADED FIREARMS IN PUBLIC, AND IT WAS DESIGNED TO DISARM THE BLACK PANTHER PARTY.

BILL AB-1591 WAS SUPPORTED BY MANY CALIFORNIA POLITICIANS, INCLUDING GOVERNOR RONALD REAGAN.

I'VE BEEN THINKING, WE NEED TO DO SOMETHING TO GET MORE PUBLICITY--TO SPREAD THE WORD TO THE PEOPLE--AND THIS IS IT.

WE GOTTA GO DOWN TO THE CAPITOL IN A SHOW OF FORCE, WITH OUR GUNS LOADED, AND PROTEST MULFORD AND HIS GUN-CONTROL BILL.

THE PRESS IS ALWAYS AT THE CAPITOL, AND THEY'LL BLAST US ALL OVER THE NEWS. EVERYONE IN CALIFORNIA WILL KNOW ABOUT US. HELL, EVERYONE IN THE COUNTRY MIGHT KNOW ABOUT US AFTER THIS.

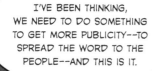

ON MAY 2, 1967, JUST SIX MONTHS AFTER THE BLACK PANTHER PARTY FOR SELF-DEFENSE WAS FORMED, AN ARMED DELEGATION JOURNEYED FROM OAKLAND TO SACRAMENTO TO PROTEST THE PROPOSED BILL AB-1591.

BECAUSE HE WAS ON PROBATION FOR A PRIOR ASSAULT CHARGE, IT WAS DECIDED THAT HUEY NEWTON WOULD NOT BE PART OF THE GROUP GOING TO SACRAMENTO. INSTEAD, SEALE LED THE GROUP, WHICH INCLUDED 24 MEN AND 6 WOMEN.

THE PANTHERS ARRIVED IN SACRAMENTO AS GOVERNOR REAGAN WAS TALKING TO A GROUP OF STUDENTS, WHICH WAS BEING COVERED BY THE PRESS.

WHEN REAGAN SAW THE GROUP OF ARMED BLACK MILITANTS, HE MADE A HASTY EXIT FROM THE GROUNDS OF THE STATE CAPITOL.

AS NEWTON HAD PREDICTED, THE ARRIVAL OF THE PANTHERS CAPTURED THE ATTENTION OF THE PRESS.

THE PANTHERS LOOKED LIKE AN INVADING ARMY AS THEY MARCHED TOWARD THE CAPITOL BUILDING WITH GUNS IN HAND.

THE PLAN WAS TO HAVE SEALE READ A MESSAGE KNOWN AS EXECUTIVE MANDATE #1, WHICH HAD BEEN WRITTEN BY NEWTON. BEFORE THE DAY WAS OVER, SEALE WOULD DELIVER THE MESSAGE MORE THAN ONCE.

PREPARED TO DELIVER EXECUTIVE MANDATE #1 AND PROTEST BILL AB-1591 BEFORE THE STATE ASSEMBLY, THE PANTHERS ENTERED THE CAPITOL BUILDING...

...AND THEY IMMEDIATELY GOT LOST WHILE LOOKING FOR THE ASSEMBLY CHAMBER.

I THINK IT'S THIS WAY.

WAIT...

...MAYBE IT'S BACK THIS WAY.

LET'S GO THIS WAY.

WE ALREADY WENT THAT WAY.

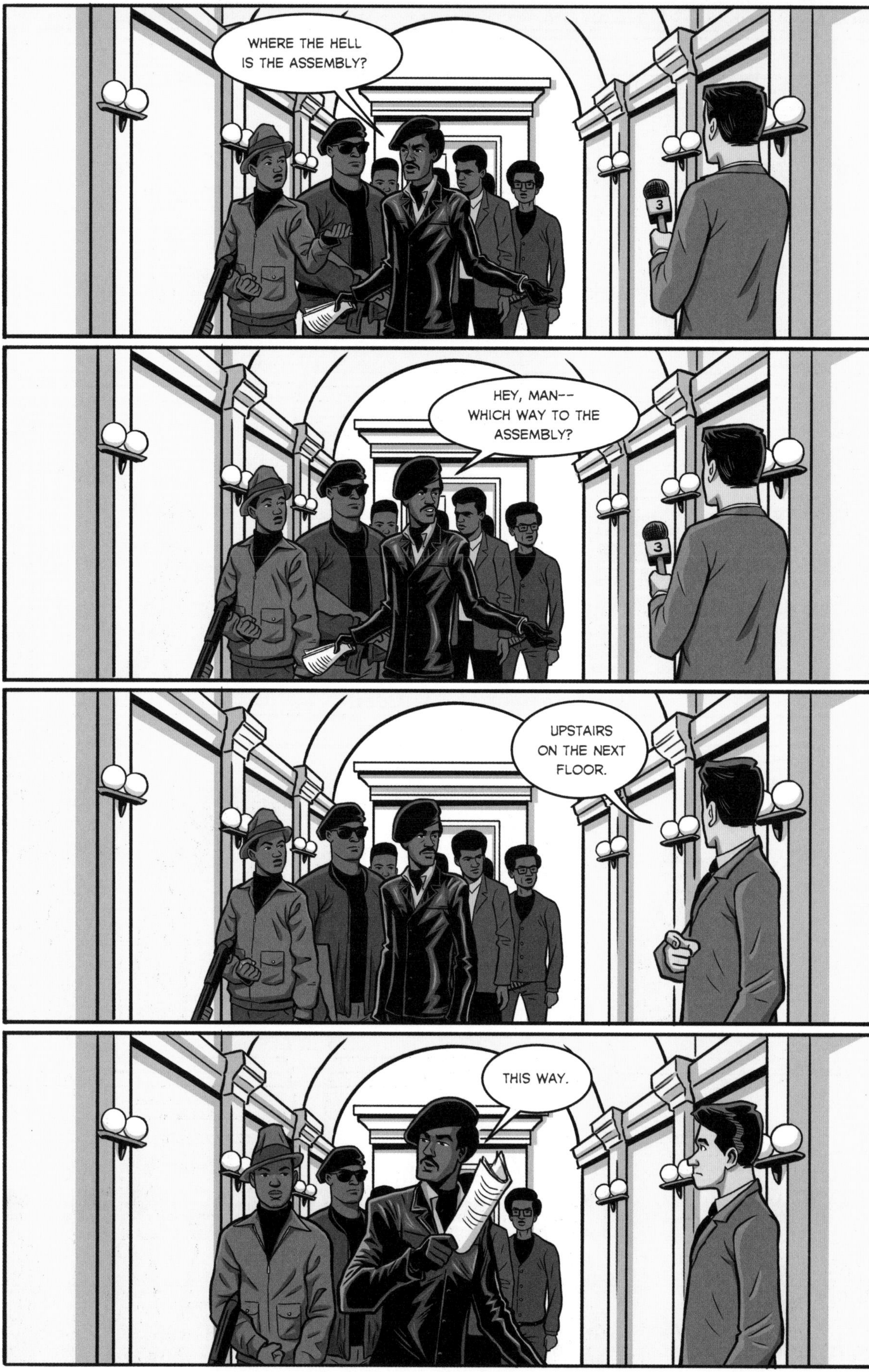
WHERE THE HELL IS THE ASSEMBLY?
HEY, MAN-- WHICH WAY TO THE ASSEMBLY?
UPSTAIRS ON THE NEXT FLOOR.
THIS WAY.

THE PANTHERS HAD BEEN LOOKING FOR THE VIEWING AREA OF THE ASSEMBLY CHAMBER, WHERE THE PUBLIC WAS ALLOWED TO WATCH AS BILLS LIKE AB-1591 WERE INTRODUCED.

IT HAS TO BE THROUGH THIS DOOR.

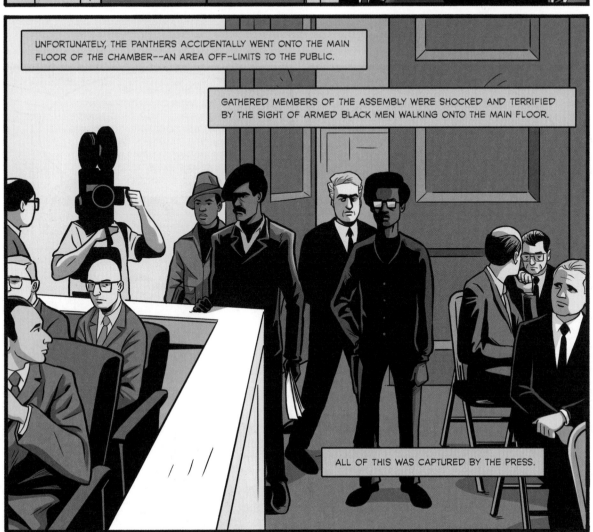

UNFORTUNATELY, THE PANTHERS ACCIDENTALLY WENT ONTO THE MAIN FLOOR OF THE CHAMBER--AN AREA OFF-LIMITS TO THE PUBLIC.

GATHERED MEMBERS OF THE ASSEMBLY WERE SHOCKED AND TERRIFIED BY THE SIGHT OF ARMED BLACK MEN WALKING ONTO THE MAIN FLOOR.

ALL OF THIS WAS CAPTURED BY THE PRESS.

OUTSIDE OF THE CAPITOL BUILDING, REPORTERS AND TELEVISION NEWS CREWS SURROUNDED THE PANTHERS, WANTING TO KNOW MORE ABOUT THE ARMED BLACK MEN THAT HAD JUST SEEMINGLY INVADED THE ASSEMBLY.

HAVING CAPTURED EVERYONE'S ATTENTION, BOBBY SEALE DELIVERED EXECUTIVE MANDATE #1 FOR A SECOND TIME, WITH THE MEDIA RECORDING HIS EVERY WORD.

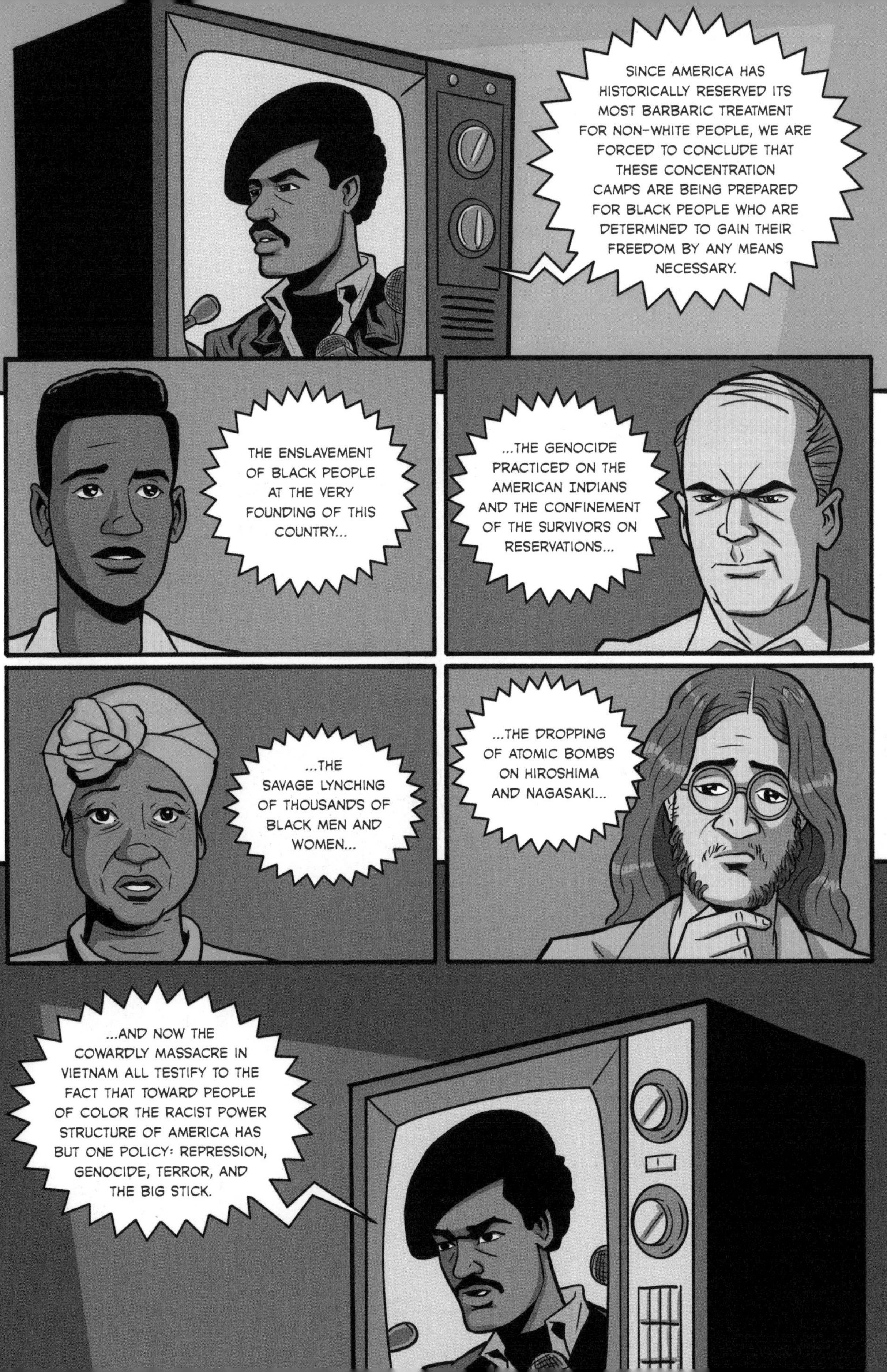
SINCE AMERICA HAS HISTORICALLY RESERVED ITS MOST BARBARIC TREATMENT FOR NON-WHITE PEOPLE, WE ARE FORCED TO CONCLUDE THAT THESE CONCENTRATION CAMPS ARE BEING PREPARED FOR BLACK PEOPLE WHO ARE DETERMINED TO GAIN THEIR FREEDOM BY ANY MEANS NECESSARY.
THE ENSLAVEMENT OF BLACK PEOPLE AT THE VERY FOUNDING OF THIS COUNTRY...
...THE GENOCIDE PRACTICED ON THE AMERICAN INDIANS AND THE CONFINEMENT OF THE SURVIVORS ON RESERVATIONS...
...THE SAVAGE LYNCHING OF THOUSANDS OF BLACK MEN AND WOMEN...
...THE DROPPING OF ATOMIC BOMBS ON HIROSHIMA AND NAGASAKI...
...AND NOW THE COWARDLY MASSACRE IN VIETNAM ALL TESTIFY TO THE FACT THAT TOWARD PEOPLE OF COLOR THE RACIST POWER STRUCTURE OF AMERICA HAS BUT ONE POLICY: REPRESSION, GENOCIDE, TERROR, AND THE BIG STICK.

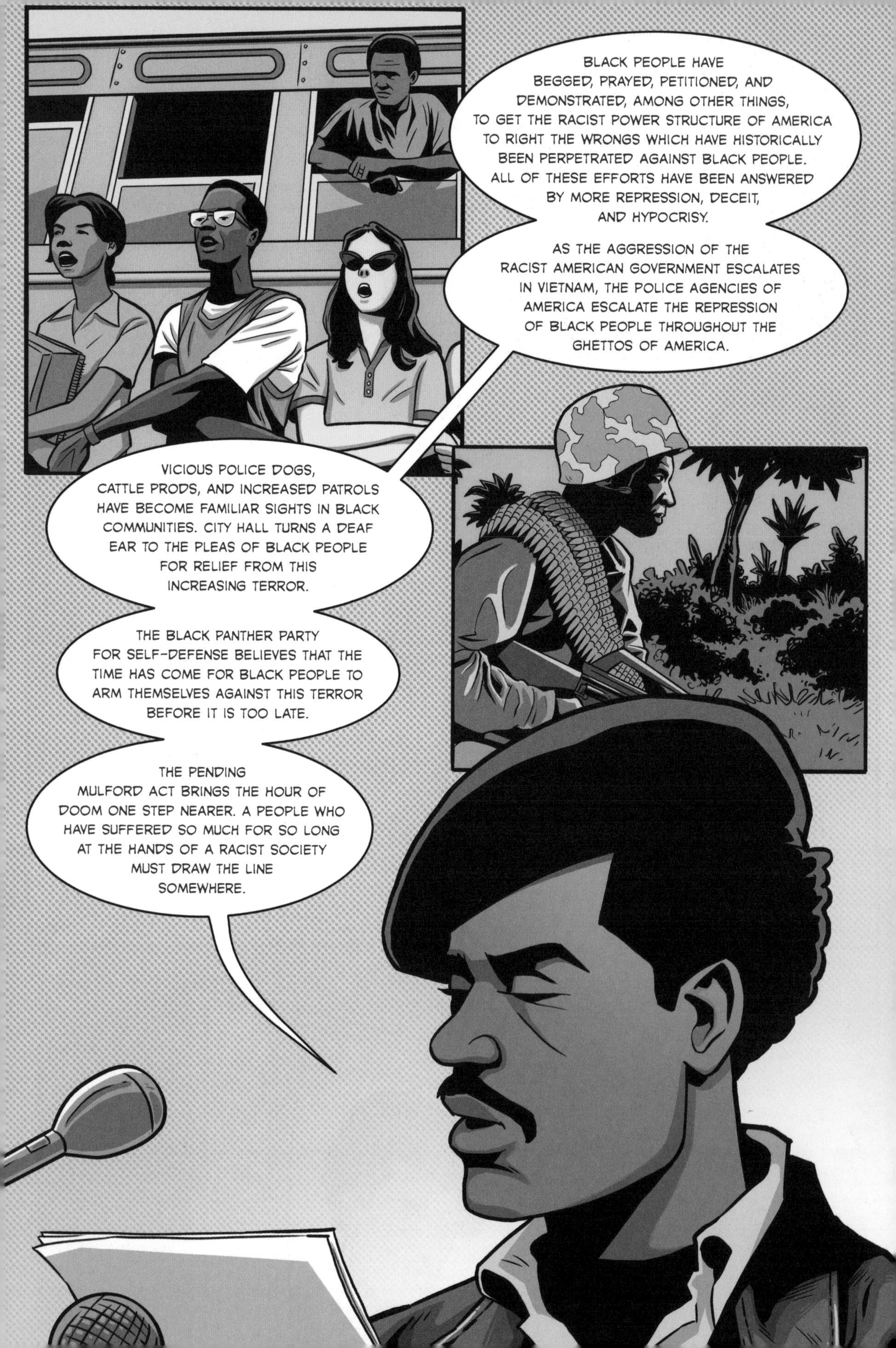
BLACK PEOPLE HAVE BEGGED, PRAYED, PETITIONED, AND DEMONSTRATED, AMONG OTHER THINGS, TO GET THE RACIST POWER STRUCTURE OF AMERICA TO RIGHT THE WRONGS WHICH HAVE HISTORICALLY BEEN PERPETRATED AGAINST BLACK PEOPLE. ALL OF THESE EFFORTS HAVE BEEN ANSWERED BY MORE REPRESSION, DECEIT, AND HYPOCRISY.
AS THE AGGRESSION OF THE RACIST AMERICAN GOVERNMENT ESCALATES IN VIETNAM, THE POLICE AGENCIES OF AMERICA ESCALATE THE REPRESSION OF BLACK PEOPLE THROUGHOUT THE GHETTOS OF AMERICA.
VICIOUS POLICE DOGS, CATTLE PRODS, AND INCREASED PATROLS HAVE BECOME FAMILIAR SIGHTS IN BLACK COMMUNITIES. CITY HALL TURNS A DEAF EAR TO THE PLEAS OF BLACK PEOPLE FOR RELIEF FROM THIS INCREASING TERROR.
THE BLACK PANTHER PARTY FOR SELF-DEFENSE BELIEVES THAT THE TIME HAS COME FOR BLACK PEOPLE TO ARM THEMSELVES AGAINST THIS TERROR BEFORE IT IS TOO LATE.
THE PENDING MULFORD ACT BRINGS THE HOUR OF DOOM ONE STEP NEARER. A PEOPLE WHO HAVE SUFFERED SO MUCH FOR SO LONG AT THE HANDS OF A RACIST SOCIETY MUST DRAW THE LINE SOMEWHERE.

WE BELIEVE THAT THE BLACK COMMUNITIES OF AMERICA MUST RISE UP AS ONE MAN TO HALT THE PROGRESSION OF A TREND THAT LEADS INEVITABLY TO THEIR TOTAL DESTRUCTION.

JUST AS HUEY NEWTON HAD HOPED, THE PANTHERS' PROTEST IN SACRAMENTO MADE THE NATIONAL NEWS.

THE SACRAMENTO BEE

CAPITOL IS INVADED

Press Corps

State Police Halt Armed Negro Band

ARMED NEGROES PROTEST GUN BILL

30 Black Panthers Invade Sacramento Legislature

RAMENTO, Calif., May PI) — With

which prohibits loaded g a vehicle. The others were for questioning.
During the Capitol

THE PRESS, HOWEVER, WERE NOT SYMPATHETIC TO THE PANTHERS' CAUSE, AND IT PORTRAYED THEM AS A HOSTILE FORCE.

POLITICIANS USED THE ACTIONS OF THE PANTHERS TO HELP PUSH THROUGH AB-1591, ALSO KNOWN AS THE MULFORD ACT--THE MOST RESTRICTIVE GUN CONTROL LAWS IN THE NATION AT THE TIME.

THERE IS NO REASON FOR LAW-ABIDING CITIZENS TO BE WALKING THE STREETS WITH LOADED GUNS.

GOVERNOR REAGAN SIGNED THE MULFORD ACT INTO LAW ON JULY 28, 1967, EFFECTIVELY TAKING AWAY THE PANTHERS' RIGHT TO OPENLY CARRY LOADED GUNS IN CALIFORNIA.

BUT NO GUN-CONTROL LAW COULD STOP WHAT HAD HAPPENED WHEN BLACK PEOPLE ACROSS AMERICA SAW THE NEWS REPORTS OF THE PANTHERS IN SACRAMENTO.

THE SACRAMENTO INCIDENT WOULD PROVE TO BE AN EFFECTIVE RECRUITING TOOL FOR THE PANTHERS ON A NATIONAL LEVEL.

UNFORTUNATELY, IT WAS ALSO USED TO PORTRAY THE PANTHERS AS A THREAT TO AMERICA.

WITHIN MINUTES OF LEAVING THE STATE CAPITOL, SACRAMENTO POLICE PULLED THE PANTHERS OVER AT A GAS STATION. WITH TELEVISION NEWS CREWS WATCHING, THE POLICE LOOKED FOR ILLEGAL WEAPONS.

THIS LOOKS LIKE A SAWED-OFF SHOTGUN.

THAT AIN'T NO SAWED-OFF, THAT'S A RIOT GUN, JUST LIKE YOURS.

HAVING FOUND NO ILLEGAL GUNS, POLICE ARRESTED MORE THAN 20 PEOPLE--SOME OF THEM NOT EVEN PANTHERS--CITING THE VIOLATION OF A FISH AND GAME CODE PROHIBITING THE CARRYING OF LOADED FIREARMS IN CARS.

AMONG THOSE ARRESTED WERE BOBBY SEALE, MARK COMFORT, AND AN UNAFFILIATED BLACK WOMAN WHO HAD BEEN BUYING GAS.

THE ARRESTS FOLLOWING THE SACRAMENTO INCIDENT WERE THE BEGINNING OF A NEVER-ENDING CYCLE OF PANTHERS GOING TO JAIL.

THE LONG, HOT SUMMER OF 1967

THE LONG, HOT SUMMER OF 1967 WAS MORE THAN JUST A SUMMER--IT WAS NEARLY A YEAR'S WORTH OF RACIAL UNREST, VIOLENCE, AND RIOTS. THERE WERE MORE THAN 150 CASES OF CIVIL UNREST IN THE U.S. IN 1967.

ACROSS AMERICA, CITIES AND TOWNS WENT UP IN FLAMES AS CITIZENS--MOST OF THEM BLACK--CLASHED WITH POLICE AND THE MILITARY. IN NEWARK, NJ, FOUR DAYS OF RIOTING LED TO 23 DEATHS. IN DETROIT, FIVE DAYS OF CIVIL UNREST LED TO 43 DEATHS, INCLUDING THAT OF TANYA BLANDING, A 4-YEAR-OLD KILLED BY GUNFIRE FROM A NATIONAL GUARDSMAN.

AS WITH THE 1965 UPRISING IN WATTS, THE VAST MAJORITY OF THE "RACE RIOTS" OF 1967 BEGAN IN REACTION TO POLICE VIOLENCE AGAINST BLACK AMERICANS.

THE KERNER REPORT

WHILE THE CITY OF DETROIT WAS STILL BURNING, PRESIDENT LYNDON B. JOHNSON APPOINTED AN 11-MEMBER PRESIDENTIAL COMMISSION TO INVESTIGATE THE CAUSES OF THE 1967 RIOTS.

JOHNSON WANTED THREE QUESTIONS ANSWERED: WHAT HAPPENED? WHY DID IT HAPPEN? WHAT CAN BE DONE TO PREVENT IT FROM HAPPENING AGAIN?

LED BY GOVERNOR OTTO KERNER, JR. OF ILLINOIS, THE KERNER COMMISSION BEGAN ITS COMPREHENSIVE INVESTIGATION INTO THE RIOTS.

SEVEN MONTHS LATER, ON FEBRUARY 29, 1968, THE COMMISSION RELEASED ITS FINDINGS--THE KERNER REPORT.

AT 426 PAGES, THE KERNER REPORT WAS AN UNFLINCHING EXAMINATION OF RACE IN AMERICA THAT CAME TO A VERY CLEAR AND DIRE CONCLUSION: "OUR NATION IS MOVING TOWARD TWO SOCIETIES, ONE BLACK, ONE WHITE--SEPARATE AND UNEQUAL."

MORE THAN 2 MILLION COPIES OF THE KERNER REPORT WERE SOLD. WITHIN ITS PAGES WERE EXPLANATIONS OF WHAT HAD CAUSED THE NUMEROUS UPRISINGS THROUGHOUT AMERICA--POVERTY, RACIAL DISCRIMINATION, LACK OF OPPORTUNITY, POLICE BRUTALITY.

THE REPORT WAS A SCATHING CONDEMNATION OF WHITE AMERICA. "WHAT WHITE AMERICANS HAVE NEVER FULLY UNDERSTOOD BUT WHAT THE NEGRO CAN NEVER FORGET--IS THAT WHITE SOCIETY IS DEEPLY IMPLICATED IN THE GHETTO. WHITE INSTITUTIONS CREATED IT, WHITE INSTITUTIONS MAINTAIN IT, AND WHITE SOCIETY CONDONES IT."

THE REPORT CONTAINED THE COMMISSION'S RECOMMENDATIONS FOR WHAT COULD BE DONE TO CHANGE THE COURSE OF AMERICA'S RACIST PRACTICES. THOSE RECOMMENDATIONS WERE ALL IGNORED.

THE COMPLETE TEXT

U.S. RIOT COMMISSION REPORT
WHAT HAPPENED?
WHY DID IT HAPPEN?
WHAT CAN BE DONE?
REPORT OF THE NATIONAL ADVISORY COMMISSION ON CIVIL DISORDERS
SPECIAL INTRODUCTION BY TOM WICKER OF The New York Times
WITH 32 PAGES OF SE...

THE BLACK PANTHER PARTY HAD BARELY BEEN IN EXISTENCE FOR A YEAR, BUT THE ORGANIZATION AND MANY OF ITS MEMBERS WERE ALREADY WELL KNOWN--ESPECIALLY BY THE POLICE OF OAKLAND.

THE OAKLAND POLICE DEPARTMENT HAD A LIST OF CARS IDENTIFIED AS BLACK PANTHER VEHICLES, WHICH INCLUDED THE CAR NEWTON WAS DRIVING WHEN HE WAS PULLED OVER BY OFFICER JOHN FREY.

FREY WAS 23 YEARS OLD AND HAD BEEN ON THE POLICE FORCE FOR LESS THAN TWO YEARS. IN THAT TIME, HE HAD ALREADY EARNED A REPUTATION FOR RACIST BEHAVIOR.

FREY PULLED OVER NEWTON AND GENE McKINNEY, WHO HAD BEEN OUT ALL NIGHT PARTYING. OFFICER HERBERT HEANES ARRIVED SHORTLY AFTER, RESPONDING TO FREY'S REQUEST FOR BACKUP. THE EXACT DETAILS OF WHAT HAPPENED NEXT REMAIN UNCLEAR, EVEN AFTER ALL THESE YEARS.

NEWTON WAS SHOT BY FREY... THAT MUCH IS CLEAR.

SOMEHOW, BOTH HEANES AND FREY WERE SHOT WITH FREY'S GUN, PRESUMABLY BY NEWTON. FREY'S GUN WAS NEVER FOUND, AND THERE WAS NO CONCLUSIVE EVIDENCE THAT NEWTON HAD SHOT EITHER OFFICER.

WHILE IN THE EMERGENCY ROOM, A WOUNDED NEWTON WAS HANDCUFFED TO A GURNEY AND ALLEGEDLY BEATEN BY MEMBERS OF THE OAKLAND POLICE DEPARTMENT.

Car Of Militant Leader Killed After Stoppin

OAKLAND, Calif. (AP) — A traffic violation led to a gun battle in which a young Oakland policeman was killed and another policeman and a leader of the militant Negro group Black Panthers were critically wounded Saturday morning, police said.

Dead is patrolman John F. Frey, 23, father of a 3-year-old daughter and member of the Oakland force for only a little more than a year.

Kaiser hospital with a serious abdominal wound Huey Newton, 25, "self-styled defense minister" of the Panthers.

Patrolman Herbert C. Heanes, a policeman since February year, was shot...

A PHOTO OF NEWTON IN THE HOSPITAL AND NEWS OF HIS ARREST BECAME A NATIONAL STORY, HELPING TO RALLY SUPPORT FOR THE PANTHERS.

CHARGED WITH THE MURDER OF FREY, THE ATTEMPTED MURDER OF HEANES, AND THE KIDNAPPING OF A MOTORIST, NEWTON WAS HELD IN JAIL AS HE AWAITED TRIAL. DURING THIS TIME, THE FREE HUEY MOVEMENT BEGAN TO TAKE SHAPE.

CHARLES GARRY WAS RETAINED AS NEWTON'S LAWYER. THE SON OF ARMENIAN IMMIGRANTS, GARRY EARNED HIS LAW DEGREE WITHOUT ATTENDING COLLEGE.

A SELF-PROCLAIMED COMMUNIST AND STAUNCH CIVIL RIGHTS ADVOCATE, GARRY WOULD BECOME ONE OF THE MAIN ATTORNEYS FOR THE BLACK PANTHERS, REPRESENTING THEM IN NUMEROUS CASES.

ON SEPTEMBER 8, 1968, NEARLY A YEAR AFTER THE KILLING OF JOHN FREY, NEWTON WAS CONVICTED OF VOLUNTARY MANSLAUGHTER AND SENTENCED TO TWO TO 15 YEARS IN PRISON.

THE BLACK PANTHER PARTY HAD NOT EVEN BEEN IN EXISTENCE FOR TWO YEARS.

NEWTON'S INCARCERATION AND HIS PENDING TRIAL BECAME A RALLYING POINT FOR THE PANTHERS AND THEIR SUPPORTERS.

FREE HUEY

THIS WAS MORE THAN A CASE OF A POLITICAL REVOLUTIONARY FACING MURDER CHARGES--IT WAS ABOUT THE GOVERNMENT ACTIVELY UNDERMINING DISSENT, WITH NEWTON SERVING AS THE SYMBOL OF THOSE REPRESSED BY THE STATE.

FREE HUEY

THE FREE HUEY MOVEMENT HELPED TO SHINE A SPOTLIGHT ON AND BOLSTER SUPPORT FOR THE BLACK PANTHERS.

ACROSS THE COUNTRY, MORE AND MORE YOUNG BLACK PEOPLE WERE DRAWN TO THE PARTY AND ITS CAUSE.

BUT IT WASN'T JUST BLACK PEOPLE WHO SUPPORTED NEWTON AND THE PANTHERS. HIS CASE HAD COME TO REPRESENT MORE THAN JUST THE REPRESSION OF BLACK NATIONALISTS OR THE CIVIL RIGHTS MOVEMENT--IT HAD BECOME SOMETHING MUCH BIGGER.

IN AN ERA WHEN POLICE AND MILITARY WERE ATTACKING ANTI-WAR PROTESTORS, NEWTON'S PLIGHT BECAME A SYMBOL FOR THE REPRESSION OF RADICAL ACTIVISM IN GENERAL.

FOR A YOUNG GENERATION TRYING TO RESHAPE THE SYSTEM INTO SOMETHING MORE EQUITABLE AND JUST, NEWTON SERVED AS AN EXAMPLE OF HOW FAR THE ESTABLISHMENT WOULD GO TO MAINTAIN THE STATUS QUO.

Bunchy Carter

ALPRENTICE "BUNCHY" CARTER WAS BORN IN LOS ANGELES ON OCTOBER 12, 1942. WHEN HE WAS YOUNGER, CARTER HAD BEEN A BOXER, THEN A MEMBER OF THE STREET GANG KNOWN AS THE SLAUSONS, AND EVENTUALLY A FOUNDING MEMBER OF THE SLAUSON RENEGADES. BY THE TIME HE WENT TO PRISON, HE WAS A NOTORIOUS GANGSTER--KNOWN AND FEARED BY MANY--AND KNOWN AS THE "MAYOR OF THE GHETTO."

CARTER WAS ONE OF "THE BROTHERS OFF THE BLOCK" THAT NEWTON AND SEALE HAD HOPED TO BRING INTO THE BLACK PANTHERS. WHILE IN PRISON, CARTER MET CLEAVER, WHERE BOTH OF THEM BECAME POLITICIZED.

IN 1968, CLEAVER RECRUITED CARTER TO START A CHAPTER OF THE BLACK PANTHER PARTY FOR SELF-DEFENSE IN LOS ANGELES, A CITY THAT WAS SEEMINGLY OVERFLOWING WITH BLACK POWER ORGANIZATIONS, INCLUDING AN ALREADY EXISTING BLACK PANTHER PARTY AFFILIATED WITH SNCC AND THE LCFO.

IN MANY WAYS, CARTER WAS THE "LUMPENPROLETARIAT" THAT NEWTON AND CLEAVER SPOKE OF--THE UNEMPLOYED, CRIMINALS, AND MARGINALIZED GHETTO FOLKS WHO LIVED ON THE FRINGES OF SOCIETY.

WITH HIS GANG AFFILIATIONS, CARTER BROUGHT TO THE PANTHERS A CRUCIAL CONNECTION TO AN ARMY OF GANGSTERS WHO WERE NOT AFRAID TO FIGHT AND ALREADY HAD A HISTORY OF VIOLENT CONFRONTATIONS WITH THE LAW. IF THE BLACK PANTHERS WERE EVER GOING TO GROW INTO A REVOLUTIONARY ARMY, THEY WOULD NEED MEN LIKE CARTER TO RECRUIT, TRAIN, AND LEAD SOLDIERS IN BATTLE.

Ericka and John Huggins

BORN ERICKA JENKINS IN WASHINGTON, DC, ON JANUARY 5, 1948, ERICKA HUGGINS WAS COMMITTED TO CIVIL RIGHTS AND THE STRUGGLE FOR FREEDOM STARTING AT AN EARLY AGE. IN 1963, AT THE AGE OF 15, ERICKA PARTICIPATED IN THE MARCH ON WASHINGTON FOR JOBS AND FREEDOM.

AS AN 18-YEAR-OLD JUNIOR AT LINCOLN UNIVERSITY IN PENNSYLVANIA, ERICKA READ AN ARTICLE IN *RAMPARTS* MAGAZINE ABOUT THE BLACK PANTHERS AND HUEY NEWTON, WHO HAD RECENTLY BEEN JAILED FOR THE KILLING OF A POLICE OFFICER. THE ARTICLE CAUSED ERICKA TO QUESTION WHAT SHE COULD DO TO HELP THE STRUGGLE FOR BLACK LIBERATION--A QUESTION SHE WOULD POSE TO HER FRIEND JOHN HUGGINS, WHO WOULD LATER BECOME HER HUSBAND.

JOHN HUGGINS WAS BORN IN NEW HAVEN, CT, ON FEBRUARY 11, 1945, AND BRIEFLY SERVED IN THE NAVY BEFORE ENROLLING IN LINCOLN UNIVERSITY, WHERE HE MET ERICKA JENKINS. TOGETHER, THEY MOVED TO LOS ANGELES IN NOVEMBER OF 1967 TO JOIN THE GROWING BLACK POWER MOVEMENT THAT INCLUDED THE BLACK PANTHERS.

FIVE — 1968: Public Enemies

BY 1968, THE BLACK PANTHER PARTY FOR SELF-DEFENSE HAD GROWN WITHIN CALIFORNIA, WITH BUNCHY CARTER ORGANIZING THE LOS ANGELES CHAPTER IN JANUARY OF 1968.

CARTER WAS JOINED BY JOHN HUGGINS, WHO RAN THE LOS ANGELES CHAPTER WITH HIM.

THE FIRST CHAPTER OUTSIDE OF CALIFORNIA WAS IN SEATTLE, WA, WITH 19-YEAR-OLD AARON DIXON APPOINTED CAPTAIN OF THE BRANCH.

THE BLACK PANTHER PARTY FOR SELF-DEFENSE WOULD GROW AT A RAPID PACE IN 1968 AND 1969, WITH MORE THAN 60 CHAPTERS OPERATING IN CITIES ACROSS THE COUNTRY.

IN LATE 1968, THE PANTHERS DROPPED "FOR SELF-DEFENSE" FROM THEIR NAME AS OTHER ORGANIZATIONS USING THE BLACK PANTHER NAME FOLDED, IN PART TO CREATE DISTANCE FROM THE OAKLAND MILITANTS.

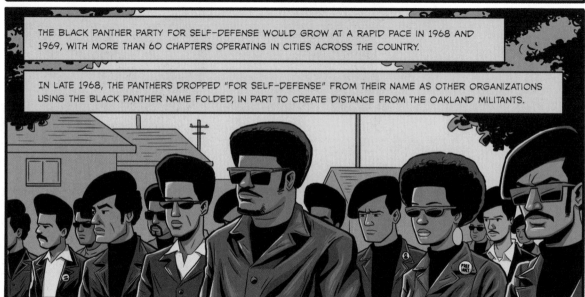

Black Panther Party Central Committee

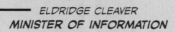

HUEY P. NEWTON
MINISTER OF DEFENSE

BOBBY SEALE
CHAIRMAN

ELDRIDGE CLEAVER
MINISTER OF INFORMATION

DAVID HILLIARD
CHIEF OF STAFF

GEORGE MASON MURRAY
MINISTER OF EDUCATION

STOKELY CARMICHAEL
PRIME MINISTER

H. RAP BROWN
MINISTER OF JUSTICE

JAMES FORMAN
MINISTER OF FOREIGN AFFAIRS

EMORY DOUGLAS
MINISTER OF CULTURE

MELVIN NEWTON
MINISTER OF FINANCE

KATHLEEN CLEAVER
COMMUNICATIONS SECRETARY

THE BLACK PANTHER PARTY OPERATED UNDER A THREE-TIER STRUCTURE OF ORGANIZATION. OPERATING OUT OF OAKLAND, THE CENTRAL COMMITTEE WAS THE RULING BODY OF ALL BLACK PANTHER PARTY CHAPTERS, BOTH NATIONAL AND INTERNATIONAL. THE HEADS OF THE CENTRAL COMMITTEE WERE NEWTON (MINISTER OF INFORMATION) AND SEALE (CHAIRMAN).

REPORTING TO THE CENTRAL COMMITTEE WAS THE SECOND TIER—STATE CHAPTERS, OVERSEEN BY CAPTAINS EITHER APPOINTED OR APPROVED BY THE CENTRAL COMMITTEE. BELOW THE STATE CHAPTERS WERE THE BRANCHES ORGANIZED BY CITY, AND THEN SECTIONS ORGANIZED BY NEIGHBORHOOD.

CAPTAIN

LIEUTENANT

OFFICER OF THE DAY

SECTION LEADER

COMMUNITY WORKERS/VOLUNTEERS

RANK AND FILE

MEMBERS OF THE CENTRAL COMMITTEE AND THOSE IN OTHER LEADERSHIP POSITIONS MADE UP A SMALL NUMBER OF THE BLACK PANTHERS. THE VAST MAJORITY OF THE PARTY CONSISTED OF RANK-AND-FILE MEMBERS. THESE WERE THE PEOPLE THAT KEPT THE PANTHERS AND ITS VARIOUS PROGRAMS OPERATING ON A DAILY BASIS.

MOST RANK-AND-FILE BLACK PANTHERS WERE YOUNG--MANY JOINED WHILE THEY WERE STILL IN THEIR TEENS AND IN HIGH SCHOOL. OTHERS CAME FROM COLLEGE AND HAD DISCOVERED THE PANTHERS THROUGH NEWS REPORTS ABOUT THE SACRAMENTO INCIDENT OR NEWTON'S INCARCERATION.

FOR MANY RANK-AND-FILE MEMBERS, THE BLACK PANTHER PARTY WAS MORE THAN JUST AN ORGANIZATION, IT WAS THEIR LIFE. MEMBERS WORKED VARIOUS JOBS, FROM SELLING COPIES OF *THE BLACK PANTHER* NEWSPAPER TO PREPARING MEALS FOR THE FREE BREAKFAST FOR SCHOOL CHILDREN PROGRAM THAT STARTED IN 1968. AS THE PARTY GREW AND THERE WAS MORE WORK TO BE DONE, MANY MEMBERS DROPPED OUT OF SCHOOL OR QUIT THEIR JOBS TO DEDICATE ALL OF THEIR TIME TO PANTHER BUSINESS.

COMMUNAL LIVING SPACES KNOWN AS "PANTHER PADS" BEGAN TO FORM IN VARIOUS CITIES, WITH MEMBERS SHARING THE SAME LIVING SPACE AND POOLING THEIR ECONOMIC RESOURCES TO COVER EXPENSES.

Tarika Lewis

TARIKA LEWIS BECAME THE FIRST WOMAN TO JOIN THE BLACK PANTHER PARTY IN THE SPRING OF 1967. A 16-YEAR-OLD STUDENT AT OAKLAND TECHNICAL HIGH SCHOOL, LEWIS WAS ALREADY POLITICALLY ACTIVE WHEN SHE JOINED THE PARTY. AN ACCOMPLISHED ARTIST, HER ILLUSTRATIONS APPEARED IN SOME OF THE EARLIEST ISSUES OF *THE BLACK PANTHER*.

IN JOINING THE BLACK PANTHER PARTY, TARIKA LEWIS BECAME PART OF A RICH HISTORY OF BLACK WOMEN JOINING THE STRUGGLE FOR FREEDOM AND EQUALITY.

OTHER WOMEN BEGAN TO JOIN THE PANTHERS IN EARLY 1967, UNDERGOING A TRAINING REGIMEN THAT INCLUDED POLITICAL EDUCATION CLASSES AND WEAPONS HANDLING.

LIKE THE YOUNG MEN WHO WERE DRAWN TO THE BLACK PANTHERS, THESE YOUNG WOMEN WERE DETERMINED TO TAKE A STAND AGAINST VIOLENT OPPRESSION.

1. IDA B. WELLS 2. FANNIE LOU HAMER 3. DIANE NASH
4. SOJOURNER TRUTH 5. HARRIET TUBMAN 6. JO ANN ROBINSON
7. MARY McLEOD BETHUNE 8. DOROTHY HEIGHT

THE ROLE OF WOMEN IN THE BLACK PANTHERS WAS NOT ALWAYS ONE OF FULL ACCEPTANCE OR EQUALITY--ESPECIALLY NOT IN THE BEGINNING.

EARLY ON, FEMALE MEMBERS OF THE PARTY WERE REFERRED TO AS "PANTHERETTES," TREATED AS AN AFFILIATE ORGANIZATION, AND SUBJECTED TO HARASSMENT.

FOR MANY WOMEN IN THE BLACK PANTHERS, THE FIGHT WAS NOT JUST FOR BLACK LIBERATION, BUT FOR WOMEN'S LIBERATION AS WELL.

ALTHOUGH THE POPULAR IMAGE OF THE BLACK PANTHERS IS HYPERMASCULINE, BY 1969, IT WAS ESTIMATED THAT MORE THAN HALF OF RANK-AND-FILE MEMBERS WERE WOMEN, THOUGH ONLY A SMALL HANDFUL OF WOMEN HELD LEADERSHIP ROLES.

BUT WITH INCREASING ACTS OF REPRESSION BY LAW ENFORCEMENT LEAVING MEN LIKE HUEY NEWTON IN JAIL AND OTHERS DEAD, THE ROLE OF WOMEN IN THE PARTY BEGAN TO CHANGE OUT OF NECESSITY.

KATHLEEN CLEAVER WAS THE FIRST WOMAN TO BE PART OF CENTRAL COMMITTEE.

ERICKA HUGGINS WOULD BE THE FIRST WOMAN TO LEAD A CHAPTER OF THE BLACK PANTHERS.

JONINA ABRON TOOK OVER AS EDITOR OF THE BLACK PANTHER FOR THE BETTER PART OF A DECADE.

AS THE PANTHERS' REPUTATION FOR VIOLENCE GREW, AND ACTS OF REPRESSION BY LAW ENFORCEMENT INCREASED, WOMEN IN THE PARTY BECAME BOTH PARTICIPANTS IN REVOLUTIONARY ACTS AS WELL AS TARGETS OF THE FBI AND POLICE.

WOMEN LIKE SAFIYA BUKHARI, ASSATA SHAKUR, JOAN BIRD, AND AFENI SHAKUR WERE ASSOCIATED WITH SUCH ALLEGED CRIMES AS BANK ROBBERY AND MURDER.

Elaine Brown

BORN ON MARCH 2, 1943, IN PHILADELPHIA, ELAINE BROWN DROPPED OUT OF COLLEGE AND MOVED TO LOS ANGELES, WHERE SHE STARTED A SINGING CAREER. IN 1968, BROWN MET ERICKA HUGGINS WHO BROUGHT HER INTO THE BLACK PANTHERS.

IN 1974, NEWTON APPOINTED BROWN AS CHAIRMAN OF THE BLACK PANTHER PARTY, MAKING HER THE LEADER OF THE ENTIRE ORGANIZATION. BROWN SERVED AS HEAD OF THE CENTRAL COMMITTEE FROM 1974 UNTIL 1977.

FROM THE VERY BEGINNING, THE BLACK PANTHER PARTY HAD TAKEN INSPIRATION FROM OTHER RADICAL AND REVOLUTIONARY ORGANIZATIONS, AND OTHER ORGANIZATIONS TOOK INSPIRATION FROM THEM.

FOUNDED IN LOS ANGELES IN 1966, THE BROWN BERETS FOUGHT FOR JUSTICE WITHIN THE CHICANO COMMUNITY. BY 1968, THE BROWN BERETS BEGAN ORGANIZING FREE MEAL AND MEDICAL PROGRAMS, SIMILAR TO THOSE THAT HAD BEEN STARTED BY THE PANTHERS.

THE WHITE PANTHERS WERE A RADICAL, FAR-LEFT, ANTI-FASCIST GROUP FORMED IN MICHIGAN IN 1968 AS A WHITE ALLY ORGANIZATION TO THE BLACK PANTHERS. THE WHITE PANTHERS WERE ALSO PART OF THE RAINBOW COALITION OF REVOLUTIONARY SOLIDARITY STARTED BY FRED HAMPTON IN CHICAGO.

THE YOUNG LORDS WERE A PUERTO RICAN STREET GANG IN CHICAGO THAT WAS TRANSFORMED INTO A POLITICAL ORGANIZATION IN 1968 BY LEADER CHA CHA JIMENEZ, WHO BECAME POLITICIZED WHILE INCARCERATED.

THE AMERICAN INDIAN MOVEMENT (AIM) WAS FOUNDED IN 1968 TO ADDRESS ISSUES OF POVERTY AND POLICE BRUTALITY FACED BY URBAN-DWELLING NATIVE AMERICANS. BY THE EARLY 1970s, AIM HAD EXPANDED ITS ACTIONS TO COMBAT POVERTY AND VIOLENCE ON RESERVATIONS, FIGHT FOR LAND AND WATER RIGHTS, AND PRESERVE NATIVE CULTURE.

AS THE PARTY GREW, IT INFLUENCED RADICAL REVOLUTIONARIES THROUGHOUT THE WORLD, WHO BEGAN TO FORM PANTHER-LIKE ORGANIZATIONS OUTSIDE THE U.S.

IN LONDON, WEST AFRICAN AND WEST INDIAN IMMIGRANTS FORMED THE BRITISH BLACK PANTHERS IN 1968.

THE DALIT PANTHERS STARTED IN 1972, NAMED AFTER INDIA'S UNTOUCHABLE CASTE, THE DALIT, WHOSE NAME MEANS "DOWNTRODDEN" OR "BROKEN" IN HINDI.

IN NEW ZEALAND, MĀORI AND PACIFIC ISLANDER ACTIVISTS ESTABLISHED THE POLYNESIAN PANTHERS IN 1971.

FOUNDED IN 1971, THE ISRAEL BLACK PANTHERS WERE MADE UP OF MIZRAHI JEWS, WHO WERE MOSTLY OF NORTH AFRICAN AND MIDDLE EASTERN DESCENT.

DENIS WALKER AND SAM WATSON FOUNDED THE AUSTRALIAN BLACK PANTHER PARTY IN 1971, MADE UP OF ABORIGINAL AUSTRALIANS.

J. Edgar Hoover & COINTELPRO

FOR MANY YEARS, THE DIRECTOR OF THE FBI, J. EDGAR HOOVER, HAD BEEN GATHERING INFORMATION ON INDIVIDUALS AND ORGANIZATIONS HE DEEMED A THREAT TO NATIONAL SECURITY. THIS INFORMATION WAS USED COVERTLY TO DISCREDIT, DISRUPT, AND REPRESS VARIOUS LEFT-WING GROUPS AND THEIR MEMBERS.

IN 1956, WHILE TARGETING THE COMMUNIST PARTY USA, THE FBI FORMALIZED ITS PROGRAM OF DISRUPTION AND REPRESSION, NAMING IT COUNTERINTELLIGENCE PROGRAM (COINTELPRO).

UNDER THE DIRECTION OF HOOVER, THE FBI KEPT A WATCHFUL EYE ON VARIOUS CIVIL RIGHTS ORGANIZATIONS AND LEADERS THAT THE BUREAU DIRECTOR BELIEVED THREATENED THE NATION'S STATUS QUO.

ONE OF COINTELPRO'S TARGETS WAS DR. MARTIN LUTHER KING, JR. THE FBI ATTEMPTED TO BLACKMAIL DR. KING BY CLAIMING THEY HAD PROOF OF EXTRAMARITAL AFFAIRS, AND THEY ENCOURAGED HIM TO COMMIT SUICIDE.

BY 1967, HOOVER HAD BECOME INCREASINGLY CONCERNED ABOUT THE RISE OF BLACK NATIONALISM AND THE BLACK POWER MOVEMENT, REFLECTED IN ORGANIZATIONS LIKE SNCC AND THE NATION OF ISLAM. HOOVER ISSUED A MEMO TO FBI FIELD AGENTS, INSTRUCTING THEM TO ENGAGE IN COUNTERINTELLIGENCE ACTIVITIES AGAINST BLACK NATIONALIST ORGANIZATIONS, WHICH AT THE TIME DID NOT INCLUDE THE BLACK PANTHERS.

BUT BY 1968, THE PANTHERS HAD BEEN ADDED TO HOOVER'S WATCH LIST, AND THEY WERE THE TARGET OF WHAT WOULD BECOME THE FBI'S BIGGEST COINTELPRO OPERATION.

Airtel to SAC, Albany
RE: COUNTERINTELLIGENCE PROGRAM
BLACK NATIONALIST-HATE GROUPS

1. Prevent the COALITION of militant black nationalist groups. In unity there is strength; a truism that is no less valid for all of its triteness. An effective coalition of black nationalist groups might be the first step toward a real "Mau Mau" in America, the beginning of a true black revolution.

2. Prevent the RISE OF A "MESSIAH" who could unify, and electrify, the militant black nationalist movement. Malcolm X might have been such a "messiah;" he is the martyr of the movement today. Martin Luther King, Stokely Carmichael and Elijah Muhammad all aspire to this position. Elijah Muhammad is less of a threat because of his age. King could be a very real contender for this position should he abandon his supposed "obedience" to "white liberal doctrines" (nonviolence) and embrace black nationalism. Carmichael has the necessary charisma to be a real threat in this way.

3. Prevent VIOLENCE on the part of black nationalist groups. This is of primary importance, and is, of course, a goal of our investigative activity; it should also be the goal of the Counterintelligence Program to pinpoint troublemakers and neutralize them before they exercise their potential for violence.

4. Prevent militant black nationalist groups and leaders from gaining RESPECTABILITY, by discrediting them to three separate segments of the community. The goal of discrediting black nationalists must be handled tactically in three ways. You must discredit those groups and individuals to, first, the responsible Negro community. Second, they must be discredited to the white community, both the responsible community and to "liberals" who have vestiges of sympathy for militant black nationalist [sic] simply because they are Negroes. Third, these groups must be discredited in the eyes of Negro radicals, the followers of the movement. This last area requires entirely different tactics from the first two. Publicity about violent tendencies and radical statements merely enhances black nationalists to the last group, it adds "respectability" in a different way.

5. A final goal should be to prevent the long-range GROWTH of militant black organizations, especially among youth. Specific tactics to prevent these groups from converting young people must be developed.

— 3 —

WELL, I DON'T KNOW WHAT WILL HAPPEN NOW. WE'VE GOT SOME DIFFICULT DAYS AHEAD. BUT IT DOESN'T MATTER WITH ME NOW. BECAUSE I'VE BEEN TO THE MOUNTAINTOP.

FOR MORE THAN A DECADE, DR. MARTIN LUTHER KING, JR., HAD BEEN THE MOST VISIBLE LEADER OF THE CIVIL RIGHTS MOVEMENT.

ON APRIL 4, 1968, AFTER GIVING A SPEECH IN MEMPHIS, TN, DR. KING WAS MURDERED.

THE MURDER OF DR. KING WAS A DEVASTATING BLOW TO BLACK PEOPLE IN AMERICA.

RIOTS ERUPTED IN CITIES ACROSS THE NATION.

STOKELY CARMICHAEL CALLED FOR BLACK AMERICANS TO TAKE UP ARMS AND RETALIATE FOR THE MURDER OF LEADERS LIKE DR. KING.

FROM HIS PRISON CELL, NEWTON SENT WORD TO THE PANTHERS AND THE PEOPLE OF OAKLAND, ASKING THEM TO REFRAIN FROM VIOLENCE.

NEWTON'S BELIEFS ON REVOLUTION WERE CHANGING--HE NOW BELIEVED THAT PICKING UP A GUN AND RESORTING TO VIOLENCE WAS NOT THE ANSWER.

IN SPITE OF THE ORDERS GIVEN BY NEWTON FROM PRISON, THE BLACK PANTHERS DEBATED HOW TO RESPOND TO THE DEATH OF DR. KING.

CLEAVER DISAGREED WITH NEWTON ON HOW TO REACT TO DR. KING'S ASSASSINATION. CLEAVER WANTED REVENGE--AN EXCUSE TO START A REVOLUTION.

DEFYING NEWTON'S ORDERS, CLEAVER LED A GROUP OF PANTHERS AND NON-PANTHERS OUT ONTO THE STREETS OF OAKLAND.

CLEAVER'S PLAN WAS AS SIMPLE AS IT WAS ILL-CONCEIVED...

...HIS GROUP WOULD AMBUSH AND KILL A POLICE OFFICER, SETTING OFF AN ARMED CONFRONTATION.

BUT BEFORE CLEAVER COULD CARRY OUT HIS PLAN, HE PULLED OVER TO URINATE ON THE SIDE OF THE ROAD...

...WHICH IS WHAT HE WAS DOING WHEN THE POLICE DROVE BY.

TO THIS DAY, NO ONE KNOWS FOR SURE WHO FIRED THE FIRST SHOTS--THE POLICE OR THE PANTHERS.

WITH POLICE IN PURSUIT, THE PANTHERS FLED ON FOOT IN DIFFERENT DIRECTIONS.

BOBBY HUTTON FOLLOWED ELDRIDGE CLEAVER...

...AND BOTH MEN TOOK REFUGE IN THE BASEMENT OF A NEARBY HOUSE.

OUTSIDE, THE POLICE BEGAN SHOOTING AT CLEAVER AND HUTTON.

FROM THE BASEMENT, THE TWO MEN RETURNED FIRE IN A GUN BATTLE THAT LASTED MORE THAN AN HOUR.

THE POLICE USED SMOKE BOMBS TO FLUSH OUT THE HIDING PANTHERS.

A SMOKE BOMB FROM THE POLICE STARTED A FIRE IN THE BASEMENT.

WOUNDED, AND TRAPPED IN A BASEMENT FILLING WITH SMOKE, CLEAVER REALIZED THEY HAD RUN OUT OF OPTIONS--IT WAS TIME TO SURRENDER TO THE POLICE.

CLEAVER TOOK OFF HIS CLOTHES. IF HE WAS NAKED, THERE WOULD BE NO WAY THE POLICE COULD CLAIM HE HAD A HIDDEN GUN AND SHOOT HIM.

HUTTON WATCHED AS CLEAVER STRIPPED NAKED.

CLEAVER TOLD HUTTON TO DO THE SAME...

...BUT 17-YEAR-OLD HUTTON WAS TOO SELF-CONSCIOUS TO TAKE OFF ALL HIS CLOTHES.

INSTEAD, HUTTON TOOK OFF ONLY HIS SHIRT WHEN HE EXITED THE HOUSE.

SURROUNDED BY POLICE, BLINDED BY THE SMOKE FROM THE FIRE INSIDE THE HOUSE, GASPING FOR AIR, AND TERRIFIED, HUTTON STUMBLED AND FELL TO HIS KNEES.

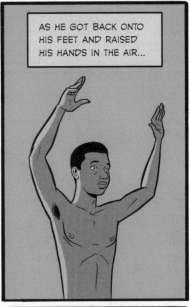

AS HE GOT BACK ONTO HIS FEET AND RAISED HIS HANDS IN THE AIR...

...THE POLICE OPENED FIRE.

CLEAVER PLANNED TO KILL A POLICE OFFICER, WHICH WOULD LEAD TO AN ARMED CONFRONTATION BETWEEN THE PANTHERS AND THE POLICE.

BUT THAT WAS THE EXTENT OF THE PLAN. CLEAVER HAD NO REAL TRAINING IN GUERRILLA WARFARE AND HADN'T FULLY THOUGHT THROUGH THE WAR HE WANTED TO WAGE.

THE POORLY PLANNED ACT OF REVOLUTION FAILED.

HUTTON, THE FIRST MEMBER RECRUITED TO THE BLACK PANTHER PARTY FOR SELF-DEFENSE, WHO HAD SURRENDERED TO THE POLICE, WAS SHOT AT LEAST SIX TIMES AND KILLED.

WITNESSES TO THE SHOOTING, INCLUDING SOME POLICE OFFICERS, CALLED IT AN EXECUTION.

MORE THAN A THOUSAND PEOPLE ATTENDED HUTTON'S FUNERAL, AND MORE THAN 2,000 WENT TO THE RALLY THAT FOLLOWED.

THOUGH THE MEDIA CONTINUED TO PORTRAY THE PANTHERS IN A NEGATIVE LIGHT, AND LAW ENFORCEMENT WAS AT WAR WITH THE ORGANIZATION, PUBLIC SUPPORT CONTINUED TO GROW.

MANY SAW THE KILLING OF HUTTON AND THE INCARCERATION OF NEWTON AS PROOF OF AN ONGOING CAMPAIGN OF OPPRESSION AGAINST BLACK PEOPLE SEEKING EMPOWERMENT.

FAMED ACTOR MARLON BRANDO ATTENDED HUTTON'S FUNERAL AND DELIVERED A EULOGY.

BRANDO WAS ONE OF MANY LIBERAL ENTERTAINERS WHO SUPPORTED THE PANTHERS.

WHILE BOBBY HUTTON WAS BEING LAID TO REST, ELDRIDGE CLEAVER SAT IN PRISON FOR A PAROLE VIOLATION RELATED TO THE SHOOT-OUT WITH POLICE.

DURING HIS TIME IN PRISON, CLEAVER ANNOUNCED HIS CANDIDACY FOR PRESIDENT OF THE UNITED STATES ON THE PEACE AND FREEDOM PARTY TICKET.

CLEAVER WAS RELEASED ON BAIL BUT CHARGED WITH ATTEMPTED MURDER. IT WAS CLEAR HE WOULD BE GOING BACK TO PRISON FOR A LONG TIME, SO HE SKIPPED BAIL AND FLED THE COUNTRY IN LATE 1968.

SEEKING ASYLUM, CLEAVER WAS INITIALLY WELCOMED IN CUBA ON DECEMBER 25, 1968.

BUT WHEN WORD REACHED FIDEL CASTRO THAT THE BLACK PANTHER PARTY MAY HAVE BEEN INFILTRATED BY THE CIA, THE CUBAN LEADER ASKED CLEAVER TO LEAVE.

FROM CUBA, CLEAVER FLED TO THE NORTH AFRICAN NATION OF ALGERIA IN THE SUMMER OF 1969, WHICH HAD NO DIPLOMATIC TIES TO AMERICA, MEANING HE COULD NOT BE EXTRADITED.

WANTED FBI

INTERSTATE FLIGHT - ASSAULT WITH INTENT TO COMMIT
LEROY ELDRIDGE CLEAVER

CRIPTION

CRIMINAL RECORD

IN ALGERIA, CLEAVER OPENED THE FIRST INTERNATIONAL OFFICE OF THE BLACK PANTHER PARTY, WHICH WOULD BECOME THE HOME BASE FOR PARTY MEMBERS FLEEING AMERICA. THE BRANCH OF THE PARTY FELL MORE IN LINE WITH HIS PERSONAL IDEOLOGIES, WHICH INCLUDED A CALL FOR ARMED, VIOLENT REVOLUTION IN AMERICA.

HE WAS JOINED BY HIS WIFE, KATHLEEN, IN 1969.

Kathleen Cleaver

THE DAUGHTER OF COLLEGE PROFESSOR AND U.S. AMBASSADOR ERNEST NEAL, KATHLEEN NEAL WAS BORN ON MAY 13, 1945, IN TEXAS. WHEN SHE WAS A CHILD, SHE AND HER PARENTS SPENT TIME LIVING IN INDIA, LIBERIA, AND THE PHILIPPINES.

WHILE IN COLLEGE, KATHLEEN BECAME POLITICALLY ACTIVE, LEAVING SCHOOL TO WORK AS A SECRETARY FOR SNCC IN 1966. IN MARCH OF 1967, WHILE ORGANIZING A BLACK STUDENT CONFERENCE IN TENNESSEE, SHE MET ELDRIDGE CLEAVER, WHO WAS SPEAKING AT THE CONFERENCE. THE TWO QUICKLY FELL IN LOVE.

WHEN NEWTON WAS ARRESTED FOR KILLING OFFICER JOHN FREY, ELDRIDGE ASKED KATHLEEN TO HELP ORGANIZE THE PANTHERS' FREE HUEY CAMPAIGN. WITHIN A MONTH, KATHLEEN HAD MOVED TO SAN FRANCISCO AND JOINED THE BLACK PANTHERS.

SHORTLY AFTER, THEY WERE MARRIED. KATHLEEN WENT TO WORK ON THE FREE HUEY CAMPAIGN, PROVING HERSELF TO BE ONE OF THE MOST EFFECTIVE ORGANIZERS IN THE PARTY. SHE WAS QUICKLY APPOINTED TO THE CENTRAL COMMITTEE--THE FIRST AND, AT THE TIME, ONLY WOMAN TO HOLD A POSITION OF POWER--WHERE SHE SERVED AS COMMUNICATIONS SECRETARY.

ONCE HER HUSBAND WAS SETTLED IN ALGERIA, KATHLEEN LEFT THE U.S. TO JOIN HIM.

ALGERIA HELD SPECIAL SIGNIFICANCE FOR THE BLACK PANTHERS AND OTHER REVOLUTIONARIES SINCE IT HAD WON ITS INDEPENDENCE FROM FRANCE IN 1962 AFTER A LONG WAR.

THE ALGERIAN WAR WAS SEEN AS A MAJOR VICTORY OF DECOLONIZATION, AND IT TRANSFORMED THE COUNTRY INTO A REFUGE FOR THOSE FLEEING RACIST NATIONS. THIS MADE ALGERIA A SEEMINGLY PERFECT HOME FOR CLEAVER AND OTHER BLACK PANTHERS ON THE RUN FROM REPRESSION IN AMERICA.

GIVEN SUPPORT BY THE ALGERIAN GOVERNMENT, WHICH INCLUDED A FINANCIAL STIPEND AND AN EMBASSY, THE INTERNATIONAL OFFICE OF THE BLACK PANTHERS--AND MORE SPECIFICALLY ELDRIDGE CLEAVER--HAD CONSIDERABLE POWER.

CLEAVER'S INFLUENCE WAS NOT LIMITED TO ALGERIA. HE TRAVELED TO OTHER COUNTRIES, GARNERING SUPPORT FOR THE BLACK PANTHERS IN NATIONS LIKE NORTH KOREA AND NORTH VIETNAM, WHICH DID LITTLE TO ENDEAR HIM OR THE PARTY TO THE AMERICAN GOVERNMENT.

AND FROM HIS POSITION IN ALGERIA, ON THE OTHER SIDE OF THE WORLD, CLEAVER CALLED THE SHOTS WITH PANTHERS LOYAL TO HIM BACK IN AMERICA--PANTHERS WHO FELT VIOLENT ACTION AGAINST THE GOVERNMENT WAS NEEDED.

BLACK PANTHER
COMMUNITY NEWS

BLACK PANTHER PARTY MEMBER
WILLIAM LEE BRENT ROBBED A GAS
STATION WHILE DRIVING A BLACK
PANTHER NEWSPAPER DELIVERY TRUCK.

A SUBSEQUENT SHOOT-OUT WITH POLICE
RESULTED IN THREE OFFICERS BEING
SHOT AND BRENT BEING ARRESTED.

BRENT'S ACTIONS WERE NEITHER
AUTHORIZED NOR CONDONED BY
THE PARTY, AND THEY EXEMPLIFIED
THE SERIOUS PROBLEM OF INDIVIDUAL
PANTHERS ENGAGING IN ACTIVITIES
THAT HAD CONSEQUENCES FOR THE
ENTIRE ORGANIZATION.

RECOGNIZING THE NEED FOR MORE DISCIPLINE AND A
CODE OF CONDUCT WITHIN THE RANKS, THE PANTHERS
DRAFTED A NEW SET OF RULES DICTATING ACCEPTABLE
AND UNACCEPTABLE BEHAVIOR FOR PARTY MEMBERS.
BRENT WAS KICKED OUT OF THE PARTY IN WHAT WOULD
BE ONE OF MANY "PURGES."

PURGES AND EXPULSIONS WERE INTENDED TO KEEP THE
ORGANIZATION SAFE FROM BOTH THE DANGEROUS
BEHAVIORS OF CERTAIN MEMBERS AND THE NEGATIVE
INFLUENCE OF PROVOCATEURS. UNFORTUNATELY, THEY
BECAME WEAPONS THAT COULD BE USED IN PERSONAL
CONFLICTS THAT HAD A TREMENDOUSLY NEGATIVE IMPACT
ON THE PARTY.

THE RULES OF CONDUCT AND THE PURGES WERE
RESPONSES TO THE ORGANIZATION'S RAPID GROWTH, AS
WELL AS ITS STRUGGLE WITH ITS PUBLIC PERCEPTION
AND WHAT IT WAS HOPING TO ACCOMPLISH.

FREE BREAKFAST

BY LATE 1968, THE BLACK PANTHER PARTY FACED MANY CHALLENGES. HUEY NEWTON WAS IN PRISON. ELDRIDGE CLEAVER WAS ON THE RUN FROM THE LAW AND HIDING IN CUBA. FOR ALL INTENTS AND PURPOSES, THIS LEFT BOBBY SEALE IN CHARGE.

SEALE BEGAN DEVELOPING THE PARTY'S FREE BREAKFAST FOR SCHOOL CHILDREN PROGRAM IN SEPTEMBER OF 1968. THIS PROGRAM WAS REMINISCENT OF SEALE'S COMMUNITY ACTIVISM FROM BEFORE HE COFOUNDED THE PANTHERS.

FOR SEALE, THE BREAKFAST PROGRAM WAS AN OPPORTUNITY TO STRENGTHEN THE RELATIONSHIP BETWEEN THE PANTHERS AND THE COMMUNITY IN A MEANINGFUL AND IMMEDIATE WAY.

SEEKING HELP IN LAUNCHING THE FREE BREAKFAST PROGRAM, SEALE REACHED OUT TO FATHER EARL A. NEIL OF ST. AUGUSTINE'S EPISCOPAL CHURCH IN OAKLAND AND PARISHIONER RUTH BECKFORD-SMITH.

FATHER NEIL HAD MOVED TO OAKLAND IN JULY 1967. SEVERAL MONTHS LATER, HAVING HEARD OF THE INCIDENT WITH NEWTON AND OFFICER JOHN FREY, FATHER NEIL VISITED NEWTON IN JAIL. FATHER NEIL BECAME A SPIRITUAL ADVISER TO THE PANTHERS, AND ST. AUGUSTINE'S SERVED AS A MEETING PLACE FOR PARTY BUSINESS.

RUTH BECKFORD-SMITH WAS THE UNSUNG HERO OF THE FREE BREAKFAST PROGRAM, SERVING AS THE COORDINATOR WHO GOT THE PROGRAM UP AND RUNNING. A RENOWNED DANCER AND CHOREOGRAPHER, SHE HAD BEEN TEACHING AN AFRO-HAITIAN DANCE CLASS THAT WAS ATTENDED BY NEWTON'S GIRLFRIEND, LAVERNE WILLIAMS.

THE FREE BREAKFAST FOR SCHOOL CHILDREN PROGRAM OFFICIALLY STARTED IN JANUARY 1969 AT ST. AUGUSTINE'S, AND IT FED 11 CHILDREN ON ITS FIRST DAY. THE PROGRAM WAS SET UP TO PROVIDE NUTRITIOUS MEALS TO POOR CHILDREN WHO OFTEN WENT HUNGRY IN THE MORNING.

BY THE END OF ITS FIRST WEEK, THE PROGRAM WAS FEEDING 135 CHILDREN IN THE NEIGHBORHOOD.

BY APRIL 1969, THE PANTHERS WERE RUNNING NINE FREE BREAKFAST PROGRAMS IN OAKLAND, SAN FRANCISCO, VALLEJO, CHICAGO, AND DES MOINES, AND WERE FEEDING OVER 1,200 CHILDREN EVERY MORNING.

LOCAL MERCHANTS DONATED FOOD, WHICH WAS PREPARED AND SERVED BY PANTHERS AND NEIGHBORHOOD VOLUNTEERS OPERATING OUT OF CHURCHES AND COMMUNITY CENTERS.

AT ITS PEAK, THE FREE BREAKFAST PROGRAM OPERATED IN NEARLY 40 CITIES, WITH LARGER CITIES LIKE LOS ANGELES RUNNING MULTIPLE BREAKFAST PROGRAMS IN DIFFERENT LOCATIONS.

THE FREE BREAKFAST PROGRAM WAS SUPPORTED BY THE BLACK COMMUNITY, AND EVEN WHITE BUSINESS OWNERS DONATED FOOD.

ACCORDING TO *THE BLACK PANTHER* NEWSPAPER, IN THE 1968–1969 SCHOOL YEAR, THE FREE BREAKFAST PROGRAM FED 20,000 CHILDREN.

FREE HUEY

IN ADDITION TO PROVIDING NUTRITIOUS MEALS TO POOR CHILDREN, THE FREE BREAKFAST PROGRAM PROVIDED AN OPPORTUNITY TO EDUCATE YOUNG PEOPLE, AS PARTY MEMBERS SHARED LESSONS IN BLACK HISTORY WHILE MEALS WERE BEING SERVED.

THE LESSONS TAUGHT DURING THE FREE BREAKFAST PROGRAM WOULD BE THE SPRINGBOARD FOR ANOTHER OF THE BLACK PANTHERS' MOST SUCCESSFUL PROGRAMS--THE LIBERATION SCHOOLS.

IN THE 1950s, CIVIL RIGHTS ACTIVIST AND EDUCATOR SEPTIMA CLARK STARTED CITIZENSHIP SCHOOLS IN THE SOUTH TO TEACH READING AND WRITING TO ADULTS.

IN 1964, SNCC STARTED AN EDUCATION PROGRAM IN MISSISSIPPI CALLED THE FREEDOM SCHOOLS.

BOTH THE CITIZENSHIP SCHOOLS AND THE FREEDOM SCHOOLS SERVED AS INSPIRATION IN THE FORMATION OF THE BLACK PANTHERS' OWN EDUCATION PROGRAM.

FREEDOM SCHOOL

THE BLACK PANTHERS ESTABLISHED THEIR FIRST LIBERATION SCHOOL ON JUNE 25, 1969, IN BERKELEY. CHAPTERS ACROSS THE COUNTRY BEGAN OPENING LIBERATION SCHOOLS IN CITIES SUCH AS NEW YORK, SEATTLE, DES MOINES, AND OMAHA.

LIBERATION SCHOOLS WERE ALTERNATIVES TO PUBLIC SCHOOL, SERVING CHILDREN FROM KINDERGARTEN TO EIGHTH GRADE, PROVIDING CLASSES IN GENERAL EDUCATION AND BLACK HISTORY, AS WELL AS SOCIAL WELFARE SERVICES FOR CHILDREN AND THEIR FAMILIES.

IN 1971, THE BLACK PANTHERS OPENED THE INTERCOMMUNAL YOUTH INSTITUTE IN OAKLAND, THE MOST SUCCESSFUL OF ITS LIBERATION SCHOOLS, WHICH REMAINED OPEN UNTIL 1982.

MORE THAN THE LIBERATION SCHOOLS OR ANYTHING ELSE THE BLACK PANTHERS DID, THE FREE BREAKFAST FOR SCHOOL CHILDREN PROGRAM WOULD PROVE TO BE THE MOST POPULAR OF THE PARTY'S COMMUNITY INITIATIVES, HELPING TO BOLSTER SUPPORT FROM THOSE WHO WERE NOT OTHERWISE ALIGNED WITH THE PANTHERS' MORE MILITANT RHETORIC.

IT WAS THE SUCCESS OF THE FREE BREAKFAST PROGRAM THAT MADE IT A THREAT.

THE BREAKFAST PROGRAM PARTICULARLY CONCERNED J. EDGAR HOOVER, WHO THOUGHT IT WAS EXCEPTIONALLY PROBLEMATIC BECAUSE IT ENDEARED THE PANTHERS TO THE COMMUNITY AND SPREAD THEIR IDEOLOGY TO CHILDREN.

ON JULY 15, 1969, HOOVER PUBLICLY DENOUNCED THE BLACK PANTHERS IN A STATEMENT THAT WOULD PLAGUE THE ORGANIZATION FOR THE REST OF ITS EXISTENCE.

THE BLACK PANTHER PARTY, WITHOUT QUESTION, REPRESENTS THE GREATEST THREAT TO THE INTERNAL SECURITY OF THE COUNTRY.

THE ELECTION OF RICHARD NIXON TO THE OFFICE OF PRESIDENT OF THE UNITED STATES IN 1968 DID NOTHING TO HELP THE BLACK PANTHER PARTY.

NIXON HAD RUN ON A CAMPAIGN PROMISE OF RETURNING "LAW AND ORDER" TO AMERICA, AND HE WAS ESPECIALLY CONCERNED ABOUT THE PANTHERS--HE FELT THAT HOOVER AND THE FBI WERE NOT DOING ENOUGH TO NEUTRALIZE THEM.

AT THE TIME OF NIXON'S ELECTION, THE FBI WAS REFINING COINTELPRO TO DESTABILIZE VARIOUS CIVIL RIGHTS ORGANIZATIONS, ALL OF WHICH WERE LABELED AS BLACK NATIONALISTS. ALL TOLD, THE FBI INITIATED 295 COINTELPRO ACTIONS AIMED AT BLACK NATIONALIST GROUPS, WITH 279 OF THOSE ACTIONS DIRECTLY TARGETING THE BLACK PANTHER PARTY.

COINTELPRO ACTIONS AGAINST THE BLACK PANTHERS TOOK DIFFERENT FORMS, AND THEY WERE ORCHESTRATED IN WAYS THAT MADE IT DIFFICULT TO IMPLICATE THE FBI.

THE FBI PROVIDED INFORMATION AND RESOURCES TO REGIONAL LAW ENFORCEMENT IN AN EFFORT TO HAVE THEM CARRY OUT COINTELPRO OPERATIONS. PAID INFORMANTS WERE OFTEN USED IN ACTIONS THAT WERE NOT MEANT TO BE TRACED BACK TO THE BUREAU OR TO LOCAL LAW ENFORCEMENT.

ONE OF THE MOST DEADLY AND DESTRUCTIVE (AND THEREBY SUCCESSFUL) COINTELPRO CAMPAIGNS INVOLVED THE LOS ANGELES CHAPTER OF THE BLACK PANTHER PARTY.

THE LOS ANGELES CHAPTER OF THE PANTHERS WAS NOT THE BIGGEST IN THE NATION, BUT IT WAS FIERCE. FOUNDED AND LED BY BUNCHY CARTER, A FORMER SLAUSONS GANG MEMBER, THE L.A. CHAPTER HAD WITHIN ITS RANKS MANY OF CARTER'S FORMER ASSOCIATES.

ONE OF THE BIGGEST RIVALS OF THE L.A. PANTHERS WAS THE US ORGANIZATION (AS IN "THEM VERSUS US"). COFOUNDED IN 1965 BY RON KARENGA (AKA MAULANA KARENGA) AND ALLEN DONALDSON (AKA HAKIM JAMAL), US HAD A DEEP RIVALRY WITH THE PANTHERS THAT WAS ROOTED IN OLD L.A. GANG TURMOIL.

THIS RIVALRY WAS EXPLOITED BY FBI COUNTERINTELLIGENCE.

FBI AGENTS BEGAN SENDING LETTERS AND INFLAMMATORY CARTOONS TO BOTH THE PANTHERS AND US, HOPING TO IGNITE TENSIONS BETWEEN THE TWO ORGANIZATIONS.

SIX — 1969: Casualties of War

ON JANUARY 17, 1969, AN ALTERCATION BETWEEN THE BLACK PANTHERS AND US ERUPTED ON THE CAMPUS OF UCLA. PANTHER LEADERS BUNCHY CARTER AND JOHN HUGGINS WERE MURDERED BY MEMBERS OF US.

THE COINTELPRO ACTIONS AIMED AT PITTING THE PANTHERS AGAINST US PROVED TO BE SUCCESSFUL. EVIDENCE SUGGESTS THAT CARTER AND HUGGINS'S KILLERS WERE FBI INFORMANTS OPERATING WITHIN US'S RANKS.

THE HOSTILITIES COINTELPRO CREATED EVEN EXTENDED OUTSIDE OF THE CITY. IN MAY AND AUGUST OF 1969, TWO BLACK PANTHERS IN SAN DIEGO--JOHN SAVAGE AND SYLVESTER BELL--WERE ALSO KILLED BY MEMBERS OF US.

A MEMO SENT TO HOOVER FROM THE FBI FIELD OFFICE IN SAN DIEGO TALKED ABOUT THE VIOLENT CONFLICT BETWEEN THE PANTHERS AND US: "ALTHOUGH NO SPECIFIC COUNTERINTELLIGENCE ACTION CAN BE CREDITED WITH CONTRIBUTING TO THIS OVERALL SITUATION, IT IS FELT THAT A SUBSTANTIAL AMOUNT OF THE UNREST IS DIRECTLY ATTRIBUTABLE TO THIS PROGRAM."

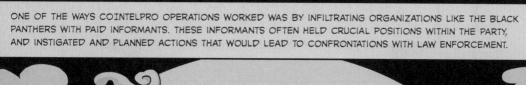

ONE OF THE WAYS COINTELPRO OPERATIONS WORKED WAS BY INFILTRATING ORGANIZATIONS LIKE THE BLACK PANTHERS WITH PAID INFORMANTS. THESE INFORMANTS OFTEN HELD CRUCIAL POSITIONS WITHIN THE PARTY, AND INSTIGATED AND PLANNED ACTIONS THAT WOULD LEAD TO CONFRONTATIONS WITH LAW ENFORCEMENT.

FBI OPERATIVES WOULD FILE REPORTS WITH THEIR SUPERVISORS, WHO WOULD THEN SHARE INFORMATION WITH LOCAL LAW ENFORCEMENT, LEAVING IT TO THE POLICE TO CARRY OUT ACTIONS AGAINST THE PANTHERS. THIS ALLOWED THE FBI TO OPERATE SECRETLY.

ANOTHER HIGHLY EFFECTIVE TACTIC USED TO DESTABILIZE AND NEUTRALIZE THE PANTHERS WAS CAPTURING THEM IN PROTRACTED LEGAL BATTLES--THE RESULT OF BEING TARGETED BY LOCAL LAW ENFORCEMENT--THAT DRAINED THEIR FINANCIAL RESOURCES AND KEPT PARTY LEADERSHIP IN A STATE OF UNCERTAINTY.

Geronimo Pratt

BORN IN LOUISIANA, ELMER "GERONIMO" PRATT JOINED THE ARMY IN 1965, AT THE AGE OF 17. BY THE TIME HE WAS 21, PRATT WAS A DECORATED VETERAN OF THE WAR IN VIETNAM, WITH 18 COMBAT DECORATIONS THAT INCLUDED A PURPLE HEART, A BRONZE STAR, AND A SILVER STAR.

AFTER HIS FIRST TOUR OF DUTY, PRATT WAS DEPLOYED TO DETROIT TO HELP STOP RIOTING DURING THE LONG, HOT SUMMER OF 1967. IT WAS THERE THAT HE STARTED TO BECOME DISILLUSIONED WITH AMERICA. AND THAT FEELING INTENSIFIED WHEN HE RETURNED TO VIETNAM FOR A SECOND TOUR OF DUTY.

AFTER RETURNING FROM VIETNAM FOR THE SECOND TIME, PRATT WENT TO LOS ANGELES, WHERE HE ENROLLED AT UCLA UNDER THE G.I. BILL. IN LOS ANGELES, PRATT MET JOHN HUGGINS AND BUNCHY CARTER, WHO RECRUITED THE VETERAN AND SOON HAD HIM TRAINING MEMBERS OF THE BLACK PANTHERS.

EAU

INVESTIGATIVE PERIOD

DATE 6/21/70

WITHIN A YEAR, PRATT WAS ONE OF THE MOST POWERFUL MEN IN THE PARTY, MAKING HIM A TARGET OF THE FBI AND THE LOS ANGELES POLICE DEPARTMENT (LAPD). AWAITING TRIAL ON MULTIPLE CHARGES, HE SKIPPED BAIL AND WENT UNDERGROUND IN AUGUST 1970.

IN DECEMBER 1970, PRATT WAS CAUGHT IN TEXAS AND RETURNED TO CALIFORNIA, WHERE, TO HIS SURPRISE, HE WAS CHARGED IN THE 1968 MURDER OF CAROLINE OLSEN. THE CHARGE WAS PART OF A JOINT COINTELPRO ACTION BETWEEN FEDERAL AND LOCAL LAW ENFORCEMENT DESIGNED TO NEUTRALIZE PRATT THROUGH FALSE AND SUPPRESSED EVIDENCE. THE PLAN WORKED, AND HE WAS CONVICTED OF MURDER.

LA 157-3436

It is noted that PRATT' included in the Black Nationalist

For the information of of PRATT's adamant expression o enforcement personnel in general, being given to reinterview PRATT development as a PRI. It is noted, consideration is given to the pos utilization of counterintelligence being directed toward neutralizing BPP Functionary.

It is noted that the inv of this report overlaps that of re view of the fact that activities oc submission of referenced report after submission of referenced re

This report is being cla because it contains information f of continuing value and disclosur could result in their identificatio the Internal Security of the Unit

LEADS

LOS ANGELES

AT LOS ANGELES, CALIFORNIA: Will continue to follow and report activities of Elmer Pratt in view of his being the BPP Deputy Minister of Defense.

INFORMANTS   LOCATION

THE NEW YORK 21

ON APRIL 2, 1969, THE NEW YORK POLICE DEPARTMENT ARRESTED 21 MEMBERS OF THE BLACK PANTHER PARTY, BASED ON INFORMATION PROVIDED BY PAID INFORMANTS.

KNOWN AS THE NEW YORK 21, OR THE PANTHER 21, THEY ALL HELD LEADERSHIP ROLES IN THE NEW YORK BRANCH, AND THEY WERE ARRESTED ON CHARGES OF PLOTTING ACTS OF TERRORISM THAT INCLUDED KILLING POLICE OFFICERS AND BLOWING UP DEPARTMENT STORES.

MOST OF THE PANTHER 21 REMAINED IN JAIL UNTIL THE END OF THEIR TRIAL, WHICH AT THE TIME WAS THE LONGEST IN NEW YORK STATE HISTORY. ON MAY 13, 1971, IT TOOK A JURY LESS THAN AN HOUR OF DELIBERATION TO ACQUIT THE DEFENDANTS OF ALL 156 CHARGES.

THE PEOPLE WILL FREE THE N.Y. PANTHER 21

THE CASE OF THE PANTHER 21 WAS NOT AN ISOLATED INCIDENT. ALL OVER THE COUNTRY, CHAPTERS OF THE PARTY WERE TARGETED BY LOCAL AND FEDERAL LAW ENFORCEMENT AS PANTHERS WERE ARRESTED ON VARIOUS CHARGES, MANY OF WHICH WERE FALSE. THIS TACTIC WAS EFFECTIVE IN KEEPING LEADERS IN JAIL AND FORCING THE PARTY TO EXPEND ITS FINANCIAL RESOURCES ON LEGAL HELP.

TENSIONS WERE HIGH IN CHICAGO DURING THE 1968 DEMOCRATIC NATIONAL CONVENTION AS POLICE AND ACTIVISTS PROTESTING THE VIETNAM WAR CLASHED FOR DAYS. A FULL-BLOWN RIOT ERUPTED ON AUGUST 28, 1968, WITH MORE THAN 20,000 COPS AND SOLDIERS GOING UP AGAINST NEARLY 15,000 PROTESTORS.

MONTHS AFTER THE VIOLENCE, ON MARCH 20, 1969, EIGHT MEN WHO HELPED ORGANIZE ANTI-WAR PROTESTS IN CHICAGO DURING THE CONVENTION WERE INDICTED ON CHARGES OF CONSPIRACY AND INCITING TO RIOT. ONE OF THEM WAS BOBBY SEALE, WHO HAD NOT BEEN AT THE RIOTS.

IN ADDITION TO SEALE, THE CHICAGO EIGHT INCLUDED ABBIE HOFFMAN, RENNIE DAVIS, DAVID DELLINGER, JOHN FROINES, TOM HAYDEN, JERRY RUBIN, AND LEE WEINER. SEALE HAD BEEN A SPEAKER DURING A RALLY BUT HAD NOT BEEN INVOLVED IN PLANNING ANY OF THE DEMONSTRATIONS.

CHARLES GARRY, SEALE'S LAWYER, WAS TO UNDERGO SURGERY DURING THE SCHEDULED TRIAL IN CHICAGO, AND HE ASKED FOR A DELAY, WHICH WAS DENIED.

WITHOUT HIS LAWYER AVAILABLE, SEALE PLANNED TO REPRESENT HIMSELF.

JUDGE JULIUS HOFFMAN DENIED SEALE THE RIGHT TO DEFEND HIMSELF.

IGNORING THE JUDGE'S DECISION, SEALE ACCUSED THE COURT OF RACISM AND DEMANDED THE RIGHT TO DEFEND HIMSELF, WHICH ONLY SERVED TO FURTHER ANGER JUDGE HOFFMAN.

SINCE SEALE REFUSED TO KEEP QUIET, JUDGE HOFFMAN ORDERED THAT HE TO BE GAGGED AND CHAINED TO A CHAIR. THIS DID LITTLE TO QUIET SEALE, WHO CONTINUED TO SHOUT THROUGH HIS GAG.

ON NOVEMBER 5, 1969, THE JUDGE CHARGED SEALE WITH CRIMINAL CONTEMPT OF COURT AND SENTENCED HIM TO FOUR YEARS IN PRISON.

THE CONTEMPT OF COURT CHARGE WAS THE LEAST OF SEALE'S CONCERNS. DURING HIS TRIAL IN CHICAGO, HE WAS CHARGED WITH A MORE SERIOUS CRIME IN CONNECTICUT--MURDER.

IN MARCH 1970, WHILE APPEALING HIS CONVICTION IN CHICAGO, SEALE WAS EXTRADITED FROM CALIFORNIA TO CONNECTICUT, WHERE HE WAS FACING MURDER CHARGES AND THE DEATH PENALTY.

SEALE'S EXTRADITION HAD BEEN APPROVED BY THE GOVERNOR OF CALIFORNIA, RONALD REAGAN.

ERICKA HUGGINS WENT TO NEW HAVEN, CT, TO BURY HER HUSBAND, JOHN HUGGINS, IN JANUARY 1969. SHE WAS 21 YEARS OLD, WITH A NEWBORN DAUGHTER WHO WAS NOT EVEN A MONTH OLD.

ERICKA STAYED IN JOHN'S HOMETOWN OF NEW HAVEN, BECOMING ACTIVELY INVOLVED WITH THE LOCAL CHAPTER OF THE BLACK PANTHERS THERE. WORKING WITH WARREN KIMBRO, ERICKA WORKED TO EXPAND THE NEW HAVEN CHAPTER.

BY MARCH 1969, THE NEW HAVEN PANTHERS HAD CAUGHT THE ATTENTION OF J. EDGAR HOOVER, WHO FELT THAT REGIONAL FBI AGENTS HAD NOT DONE ENOUGH TO NEUTRALIZE THE CHAPTER.

TO DATE YOU HAVE SUBMITTED NO CONCRETE RECOMMENDATIONS UNDER THIS PROGRAM CONCERNING THE BLACK PANTHER PARTY, DESPITE THE FACT THIS EXTREMELY DANGEROUS ORGANIZATION IS IN FOUR CITIES IN YOUR DIVISION.

HOOVER PUT PRESSURE ON THE FBI FIELD OFFICE IN NEW HAVEN TO ORCHESTRATE COINTELPRO ACTIONS AGAINST THE PARTY.

IN MAY 1969, SHORTLY AFTER THE ARREST OF THE PANTHER 21 IN NEW YORK, GEORGE SAMS ARRIVED IN NEW HAVEN. KNOWN AS "CRAZY GEORGE," SAMS HAD BEEN A MEMBER OF THE NEW YORK BLACK PANTHERS AND CLAIMED THAT HE HAD BEEN SENT TO NEW HAVEN BY THE NATIONAL OFFICE TO FIND SPIES IN THE ORGANIZATION.

SAMS HAD A BAD REPUTATION, INCLUDING STABBING A PARTY MEMBER IN OAKLAND AND ALLEGEDLY RAPING A MEMBER OF THE NEW YORK CHAPTER. AT ONE POINT, SAMS HAD BEEN KICKED OUT OF THE PANTHERS, BUT HE WAS ALLOWED BACK IN DESPITE HIS BEHAVIOR.

ACCOMPANYING SAMS TO NEW HAVEN ON MAY 17, 1969, WAS 19-YEAR-OLD ALEX RACKLEY, A PANTHER FROM THE NEW YORK BRANCH.

WITH SAMS ENCOURAGING THEM, SEVERAL PANTHERS TORTURED RACKLEY--TYING HIM TO A BED, BEATING HIM, AND SCALDING HIM WITH BOILING WATER. AFTER A DAY OF TORTURE, RACKLEY CONFESSED--EVEN THOUGH HE WAS NOT ACTUALLY A SPY.

TWO DAYS AFTER ARRIVING IN NEW HAVEN, SAMS ACCUSED RACKLEY OF BEING A SPY FOR THE FBI.

AFTER THE CONFESSION, SAMS GAVE THE ORDER TO HAVE RACKLEY KILLED.

ALEX RACKLEY WAS MURDERED ON MAY 20, 1969.

THE NEXT DAY, HIS BODY WAS DISCOVERED.

WITHIN HOURS OF RACKLEY'S BODY BEING FOUND, 14 OF THE NEW HAVEN PANTHERS WERE ARRESTED, INCLUDING ERICKA HUGGINS. SAMS WAS NOWHERE TO BE FOUND.

CONVENIENTLY, SAMS HAD RECORDED RACKLEY'S TORTURE. THE RECORDING, WHICH INCLUDES ERICKA HUGGINS INTERROGATING RACKLEY, WAS FOUND BY THE POLICE AND USED AS EVIDENCE AGAINST THE NEW HAVEN PANTHERS.

INDEX

A

C-60

SEVERAL MONTHS AFTER RACKLEY'S MURDER, GEORGE SAMS WAS CAPTURED IN CANADA.

READY TO MAKE A DEAL WITH THE POLICE, SAMS CLAIMED THAT THE ORDER TO KILL RACKLEY HAD COME DIRECTLY FROM BOBBY SEALE, WHO HAD BEEN IN NEW HAVEN THE NIGHT OF THE MURDER.

BASED ON SAMS'S TESTIMONY, SEALE WAS CHARGED WITH RACKLEY'S MURDER.

IN ADDITION TO SEALE, ERICKA HUGGINS AND 13 OTHER PANTHERS WERE CHARGED WITH THE KILLING OF RACKLEY.

IN OCTOBER 1970, SEALE AND HUGGINS WENT ON TRIAL TOGETHER. JURY SELECTION TOOK FOUR MONTHS, AND THE TRIAL LASTED ANOTHER FIVE.

THE JURY FAILED TO REACH A VERDICT IN EITHER CASE, WITH MOST OF THE JURORS IN FAVOR OF ACQUITTAL.

JUDGE HAROLD MULVEY DISMISSED THE CHARGES AGAINST SEALE AND HUGGINS ON MAY 25, 1971. ALTHOUGH IT HAS NEVER BEEN CONFIRMED, GEORGE SAMS WAS SUSPECTED OF BEING AN FBI INFORMANT. THE MURDER OF RACKLEY IS WIDELY BELIEVED TO BE PART OF A COINTELPRO ACTION MEANT TO DISCREDIT THE PANTHERS AND JAIL KEY LEADERS LIKE SEALE AND HUGGINS.

AFTER SPENDING MORE THAN A YEAR IN PRISON, BOTH SEALE AND HUGGINS WERE SET FREE.

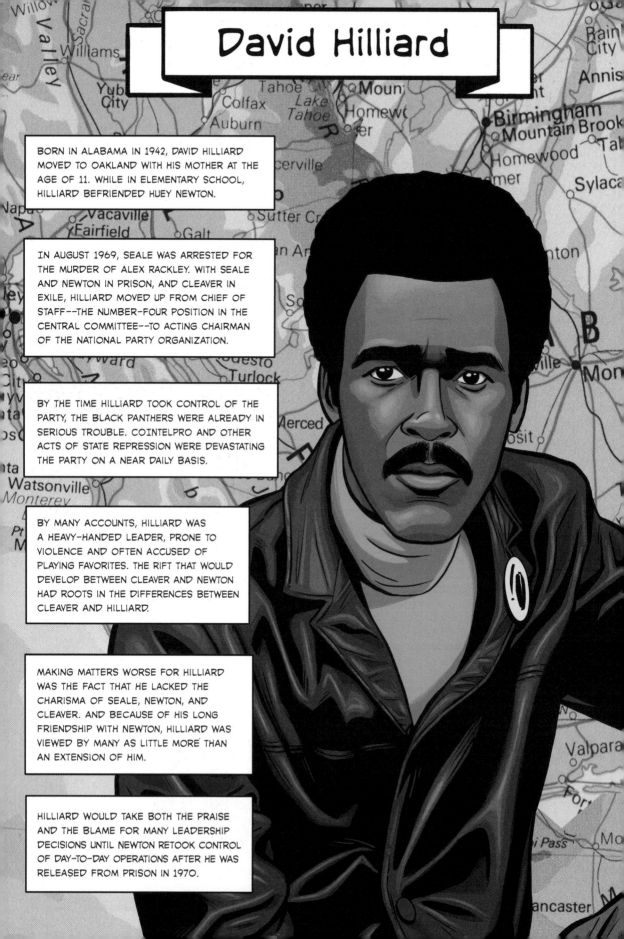

David Hilliard

BORN IN ALABAMA IN 1942, DAVID HILLIARD MOVED TO OAKLAND WITH HIS MOTHER AT THE AGE OF 11. WHILE IN ELEMENTARY SCHOOL, HILLIARD BEFRIENDED HUEY NEWTON.

IN AUGUST 1969, SEALE WAS ARRESTED FOR THE MURDER OF ALEX RACKLEY. WITH SEALE AND NEWTON IN PRISON, AND CLEAVER IN EXILE, HILLIARD MOVED UP FROM CHIEF OF STAFF--THE NUMBER-FOUR POSITION IN THE CENTRAL COMMITTEE--TO ACTING CHAIRMAN OF THE NATIONAL PARTY ORGANIZATION.

BY THE TIME HILLIARD TOOK CONTROL OF THE PARTY, THE BLACK PANTHERS WERE ALREADY IN SERIOUS TROUBLE. COINTELPRO AND OTHER ACTS OF STATE REPRESSION WERE DEVASTATING THE PARTY ON A NEAR DAILY BASIS.

BY MANY ACCOUNTS, HILLIARD WAS A HEAVY-HANDED LEADER, PRONE TO VIOLENCE AND OFTEN ACCUSED OF PLAYING FAVORITES. THE RIFT THAT WOULD DEVELOP BETWEEN CLEAVER AND NEWTON HAD ROOTS IN THE DIFFERENCES BETWEEN CLEAVER AND HILLIARD.

MAKING MATTERS WORSE FOR HILLIARD WAS THE FACT THAT HE LACKED THE CHARISMA OF SEALE, NEWTON, AND CLEAVER. AND BECAUSE OF HIS LONG FRIENDSHIP WITH NEWTON, HILLIARD WAS VIEWED BY MANY AS LITTLE MORE THAN AN EXTENSION OF HIM.

HILLIARD WOULD TAKE BOTH THE PRAISE AND THE BLAME FOR MANY LEADERSHIP DECISIONS UNTIL NEWTON RETOOK CONTROL OF DAY-TO-DAY OPERATIONS AFTER HE WAS RELEASED FROM PRISON IN 1970.

HOW THE CHICAGO BRANCH OF THE BLACK PANTHERS CAME TO EXIST

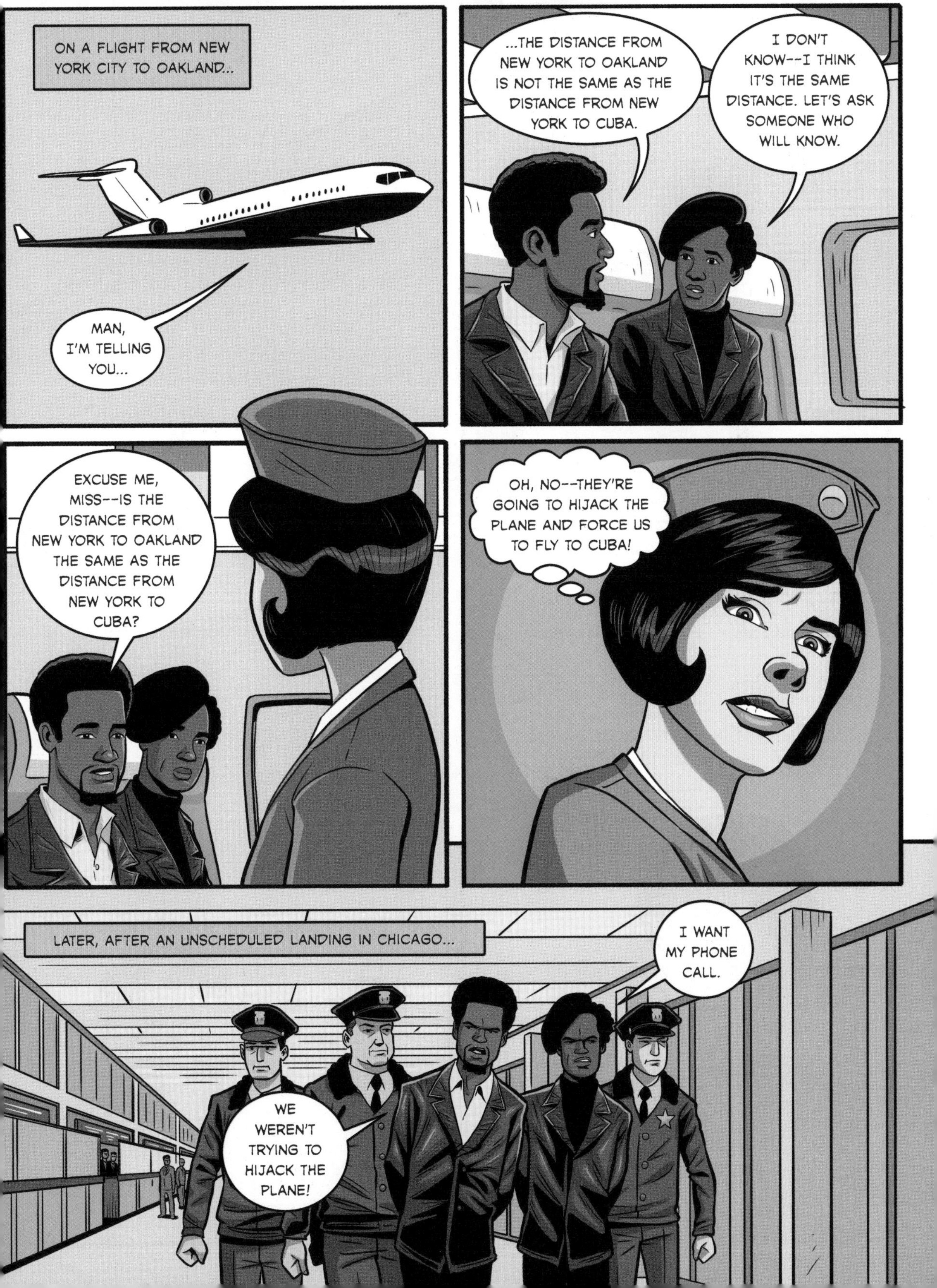
ON A FLIGHT FROM NEW YORK CITY TO OAKLAND...
MAN, I'M TELLING YOU...
...THE DISTANCE FROM NEW YORK TO OAKLAND IS NOT THE SAME AS THE DISTANCE FROM NEW YORK TO CUBA.
I DON'T KNOW--I THINK IT'S THE SAME DISTANCE. LET'S ASK SOMEONE WHO WILL KNOW.
EXCUSE ME, MISS--IS THE DISTANCE FROM NEW YORK TO OAKLAND THE SAME AS THE DISTANCE FROM NEW YORK TO CUBA?
OH, NO--THEY'RE GOING TO HIJACK THE PLANE AND FORCE US TO FLY TO CUBA!
LATER, AFTER AN UNSCHEDULED LANDING IN CHICAGO...
I WANT MY PHONE CALL.
WE WEREN'T TRYING TO HIJACK THE PLANE!

YOU WERE ARRESTED FOR WHAT?!

MAN, WE AIN'T GOT ANY PANTHERS IN CHICAGO TO BAIL YOU OUT.

LET ME SEE IF I CAN THINK OF SOMETHING.

HEY, THIS IS DAVID HILLIARD FROM THE BLACK PANTHER PARTY-- WE MET A FEW MONTHS BACK WHEN YOU WERE IN OAKLAND.

TWO OF MY MEN ARE IN JAIL IN CHICAGO, AND YOU'RE THE ONLY PERSON I KNOW THERE.

YOU WANT ME TO DO WHAT?

BOBBY RUSH WAS THE CODIRECTOR OF THE CHICAGO CHAPTER OF SNCC. IN OCTOBER 1968, RUSH HAD TRIED TO START A BRANCH OF THE BLACK PANTHERS IN CHICAGO, ONLY TO BE TOLD BY THE CENTRAL COMMITTEE THAT THERE WAS ALREADY A CHAPTER IN THE CITY.

THIS OTHER CHICAGO PANTHER BRANCH HAD STOPPED COMMUNICATING WITH THE CENTRAL COMMITTEE AFTER THEIR PHONE WAS APPARENTLY SHUT OFF, AND WITH TWO PANTHERS IN JAIL AND NO ONE TO BAIL THEM OUT, HILLIARD REACHED OUT TO RUSH.

WHILE HE WAS AT IT, HILLIARD ASKED RUSH TO START A CHAPTER OF THE BLACK PANTHER PARTY IN ILLINOIS, WITH A BRANCH IN CHICAGO... AND MAKE SURE IT STAYED IN CONTACT WITH THE CENTRAL COMMITTEE.

THE CITY OF CHICAGO HAD A LONG HISTORY OF RACISM AND VIOLENCE TOWARD BLACK PEOPLE. DURING THE RED SUMMER OF 1919, RACIAL UNREST IN THE CITY LED TO MORE THAN 30 DEATHS. RACE RIOTS OCCURRED IN CHICAGO AND SURROUNDING COMMUNITIES IN 1964, 1966, AND 1968.

POLICE IN CHICAGO HAD A BAD REPUTATION FOR VIOLENCE AND BRUTALITY. IN 1969 ALONE, THERE WERE 11 REPORTED INCIDENTS OF CHICAGO POLICE OFFICERS KILLING UNARMED BLACK FOLKS. AMONG THESE DEATHS WERE BROTHERS JOHN (17) AND MICHAEL SOTO (20), KILLED LESS THAN TWO WEEKS APART.

LIKE MANY OTHER CITIES WITH LARGE POPULATIONS OF POOR MINORITIES, CHICAGO HAD A CONSIDERABLE NUMBER OF STREET GANGS.

MANY OF THE GANGS HAD BECOME INCREASINGLY POLITICIZED, WORKING TO IMPROVE THE COMMUNITY IN WAYS THAT WERE SIMILAR TO WHAT THE BLACK PANTHERS WERE TRYING TO DO.

THOUGH THESE GANGS--LIKE THE BLACK DISCIPLES AND THE BLACKSTONE RANGERS--WERE STILL INVOLVED IN ILLEGAL ACTIVITIES, THEY HAD ALSO TAKEN THE STANCE OF PROTECTING THE GHETTO FROM THE OPPRESSIVE FORCE OF THE POLICE.

Fred Hampton

BORN ON AUGUST 30, 1948, FRED HAMPTON WAS ALREADY A COMMUNITY ACTIVIST WHEN HE WAS RECRUITED BY BOBBY RUSH TO JOIN THE FLEDGLING CHICAGO BRANCH OF THE BLACK PANTHERS IN NOVEMBER 1968 AT BARELY 20 YEARS OLD.

BEFORE JOINING THE PANTHERS, HAMPTON WAS THE PRESIDENT OF THE NAACP'S YOUTH COUNCIL IN CHICAGO'S PREDOMINANTLY BLACK SUBURB OF MAYWOOD. IN 1967, MORE THAN A YEAR BEFORE JOINING THE PANTHERS, HE WAS A KEY ORGANIZER IN A RALLY TO BUILD A RECREATIONAL CENTER IN MAYWOOD. AFTER VIOLENCE ERUPTED BETWEEN BLACK TEENAGERS AND THE POLICE, HAMPTON WAS ARRESTED.

AFTER THE INCIDENT IN MAYWOOD, HAMPTON WAS PLACED UNDER SURVEILLANCE BY THE CHICAGO POLICE DEPARTMENT. HE WAS ALSO PLACED ON THE FBI'S AGITATOR INDEX--A LIST OF ACTIVISTS THAT J. EDGAR HOOVER WANTED CLOSELY WATCHED.

WORKING WITH RUSH AND OTHER MEMBERS OF THE ILLINOIS BLACK PANTHER PARTY, HAMPTON PROVED HIMSELF TO BE AN INCREDIBLE LEADER AND ORGANIZER.

HE QUICKLY BUILT ALLIANCES WITH AN ECLECTIC MIX OF RADICAL GROUPS, INCLUDING PUERTO RICAN ACTIVISTS THE YOUNG LORDS AND THE FAR-LEFT YOUNG PATRIOTS. HAMPTON CALLED HIS GROUP OF ALLIES HIS "RAINBOW COALITION," YEARS BEFORE ACTIVIST JESSE JACKSON FORMED HIS OWN NATIONAL RAINBOW COALITION IN 1984.

HAMPTON'S SKILLS AS A LEADER AND ORGANIZER WENT BEYOND BUILDING ALLIANCES WITH OTHER POLITICAL ORGANIZATIONS; HE ALSO WORKED WITH THE BLACK STREET GANGS OF CHICAGO, STARTING WITH THE BLACK DISCIPLES.

AFTER FORMING AN ALLIANCE BETWEEN THE BLACK DISCIPLES AND THE PANTHERS, HAMPTON ATTEMPTED TO CREATE A SIMILAR ALLIANCE WITH THEIR MAIN RIVALS, THE BLACKSTONE RANGERS—CHICAGO'S LARGEST GANG.

LED BY JEFF FORT, THE RANGERS HAD MORE THAN 5,000 MEMBERS. A MERGER BETWEEN THE RANGERS AND THE PANTHERS WOULD HAVE SIGNIFICANTLY INCREASED THE MEMBERSHIP OF THE PANTHERS IN CHICAGO.

PERHAPS MORE IMPORTANT, THE RANGERS, AS WELL AS OTHER GANGS LIKE THE BLACK DISCIPLES, WERE NO STRANGERS TO VIOLENT CONFRONTATIONS WITH THE POLICE—THEY WERE FIGHTERS, AND POTENTIAL SOLDIERS FOR THE COMING REVOLUTION.

FEARING A MERGER BETWEEN THE PANTHERS AND THE RANGERS, THE FBI BEGAN A COUNTERINTELLIGENCE INITIATIVE TO CREATE CONFLICT BETWEEN THE TWO GROUPS.

IN LATE 1968, THE FBI SENT A FAKE LETTER TO JEFF FORT THAT CLAIMED TO BE FROM AN ANONYMOUS "BLACK BROTHER," WARNING THE GANG LEADER THAT THE BLACK PANTHERS WERE GOING TO KILL HIM AND HOPING THE LETTER WOULD LEAD TO A VIOLENT CONFRONTATION LIKE THE ONE THAT LED TO THE KILLINGS OF CARTER AND HUGGINS IN LOS ANGELES.

BUT JEFF FORT DIDN'T FALL FOR IT.

THE RANGERS DECIDED NOT TO MERGE WITH THE PANTHERS. THIS DIDN'T, HOWEVER, DIMINISH THE PERCEPTION OF HAMPTON AS A MAJOR THREAT BY THE FBI OR THE CHICAGO POLICE.

HAVING PROVEN HIMSELF TO BE A SUCCESSFUL ORGANIZER, AN EFFECTIVE CHAPTER LEADER, AND A FIERY SPEAKER, HAMPTON FOUND HIMSELF IN A UNIQUE POSITION ONLY A FEW MONTHS AFTER HAVING JOINED THE BLACK PANTHERS.

BY THE SUMMER OF 1969, BOTH BOBBY SEALE AND HUEY NEWTON WERE IN PRISON, ELDRIDGE AND KATHLEEN CLEAVER WERE IN EXILE IN ALGERIA, DAVID HILLIARD WAS UNDER INDICTMENT, BUNCHY CARTER AND JOHN HUGGINS WERE DEAD, AND THE ENTIRE LEADERSHIP OF THE NEW YORK PANTHERS HAD BEEN ARRESTED.

WITHOUT ANY STABILITY IN THE CENTRAL COMMITTEE, HAMPTON WAS THE NEXT PERSON TO ASSUME A LEADERSHIP ROLE AS BOTH CHIEF OF STAFF AND THE NATIONAL SPOKESMAN FOR THE PARTY. AND THIS MADE HIM A THREAT IN THE EYES OF HOOVER AND THE FBI.

THE MURDER OF FRED HAMPTON

ON THE MORNING OF DECEMBER 4, 1969, THE CHICAGO POLICE DEPARTMENT STAGED A PRE-DAWN RAID ON THE APARTMENT OF FRED HAMPTON.

NINE PEOPLE WERE IN THE APARTMENT--ALL OF THEM PANTHERS--INCLUDING HAMPTON AND HIS PREGNANT GIRLFRIEND, DEBORAH JOHNSON.

EVERYONE WAS ASLEEP.

NOK NOK

FRED?

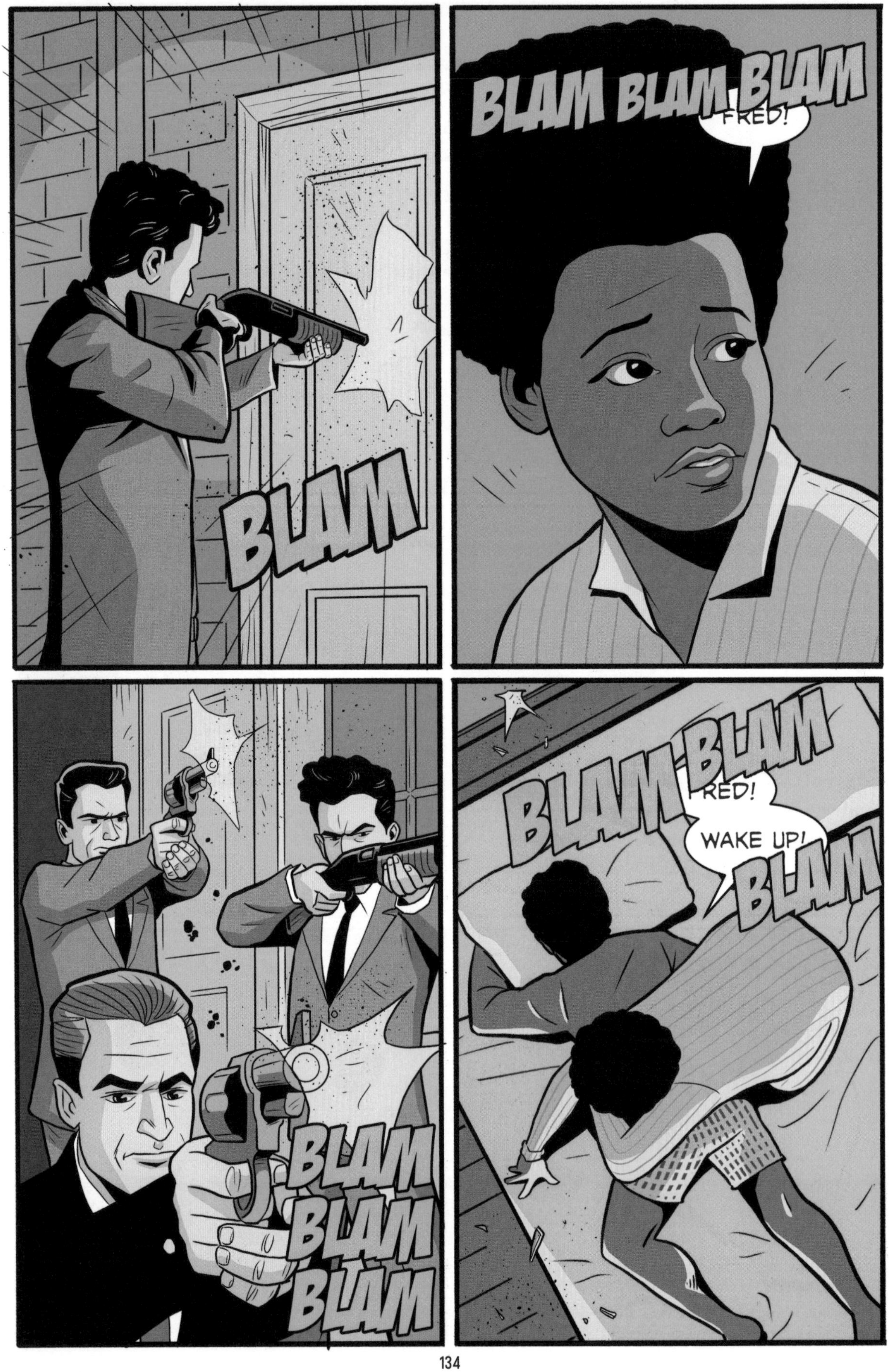
BLAM
BLAM BLAM BLAM
FRED!
BLAM
BLAM
BLAM
BLAM BLAM
RED!
WAKE UP!
BLAM

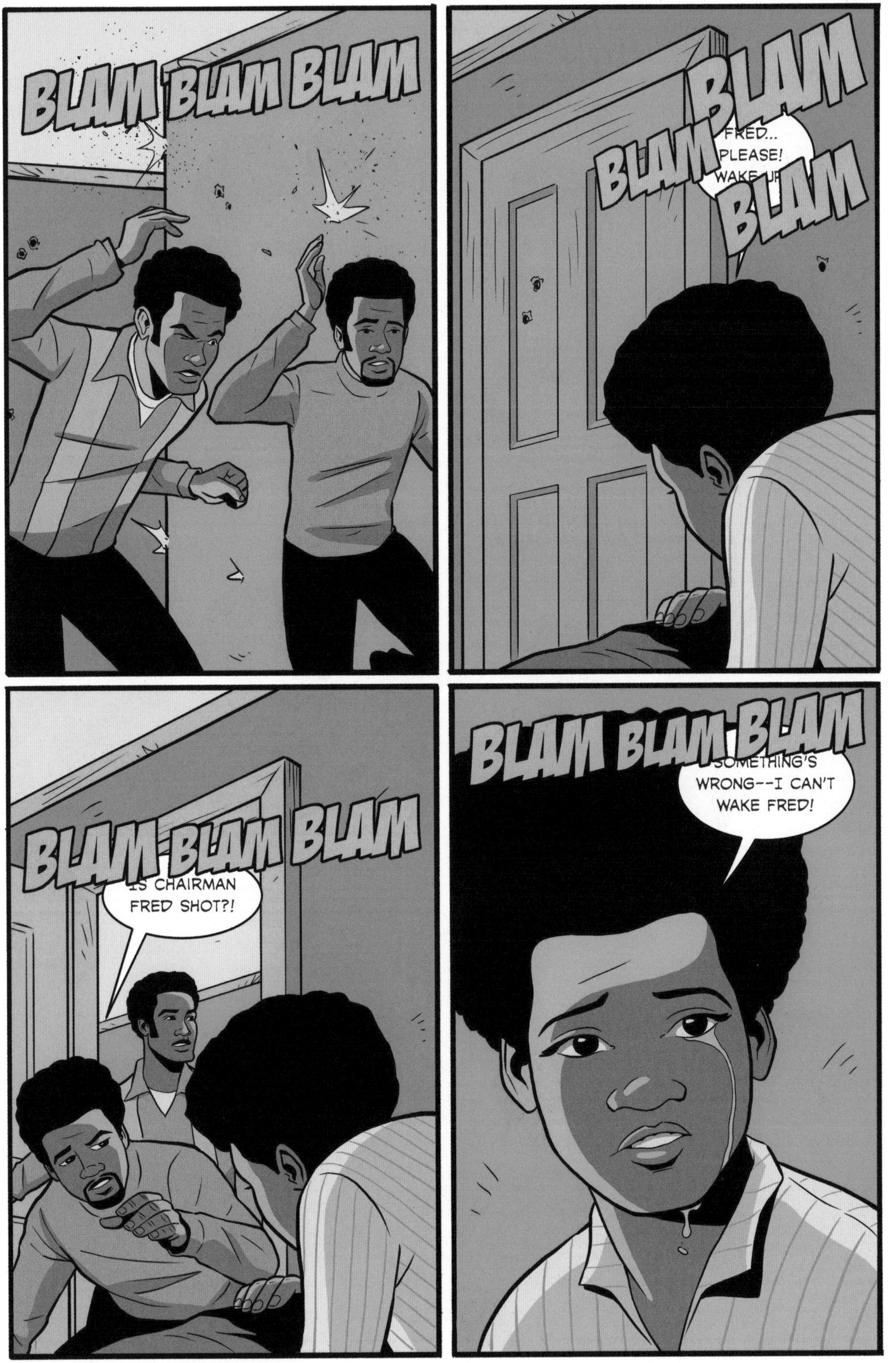

BLAM BLAM BLAM
BLAM BLAM BLAM BLAM
FRED... PLEASE! WAKE U
BLAM BLAM BLAM
IS CHAIRMAN FRED SHOT?!
BLAM BLAM BLAM
SOMETHING'S WRONG--I CAN'T WAKE FRED!

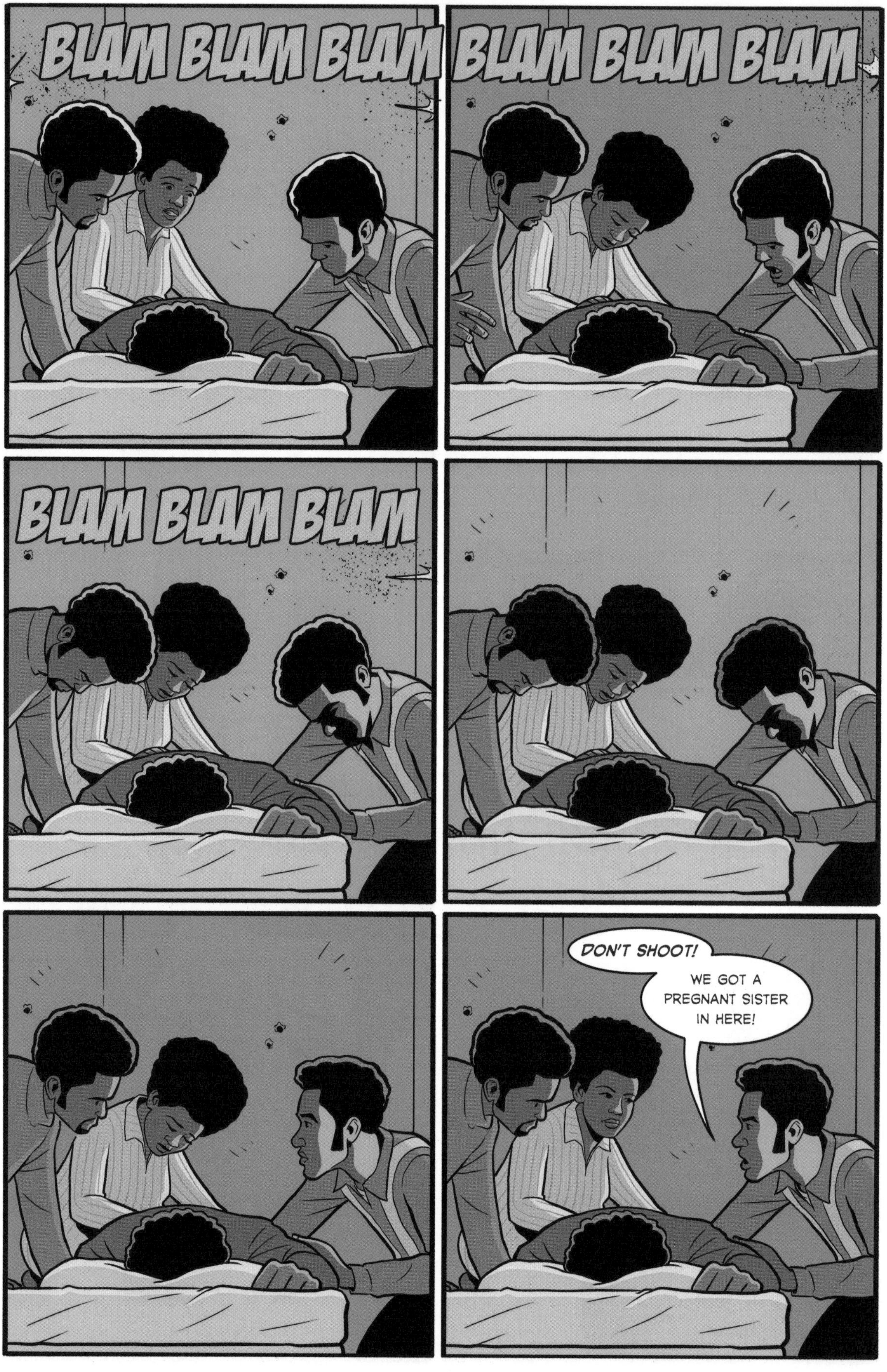
BLAM BLAM BLAM
BLAM BLAM BLAM
BLAM BLAM BLAM
DON'T SHOOT!
WE GOT A PREGNANT SISTER IN HERE!

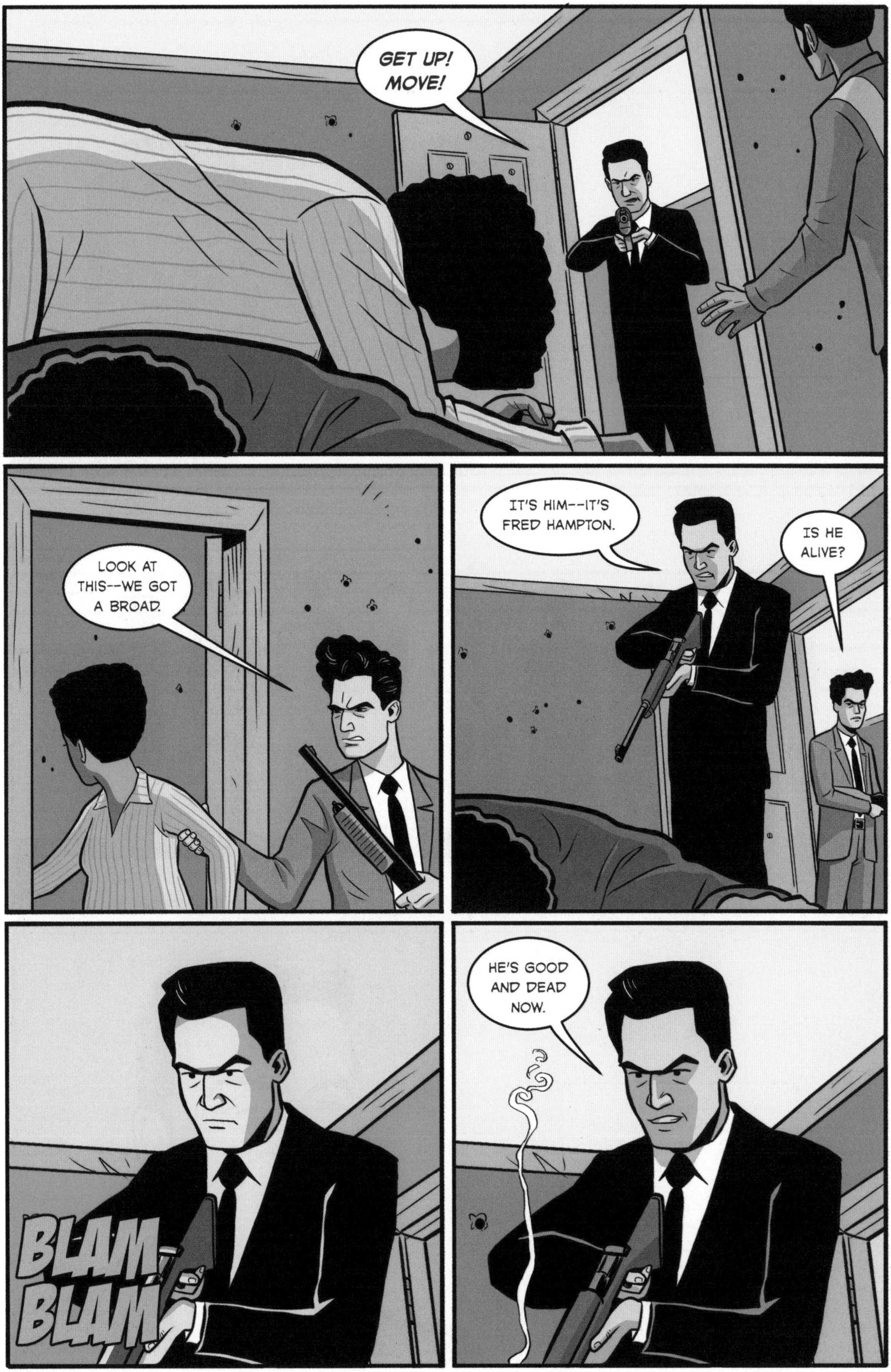
GET UP! MOVE!
LOOK AT THIS--WE GOT A BROAD.
IT'S HIM--IT'S FRED HAMPTON.
IS HE ALIVE?
BLAM BLAM
HE'S GOOD AND DEAD NOW.

GETTING AWAY WITH MURDER... ALMOST

THE POLICE CLAIMED TO BE ACTING ON A TIP THAT FRED HAMPTON'S APARTMENT WAS FILLED WITH WEAPONS.

IN THE ENSUING RAID, HAMPTON WAS KILLED, ALONG WITH FELLOW PANTHER MARK CLARK.

THERE WERE NINE OCCUPANTS IN THE APARTMENT.

FOUR OF THEM WERE WOUNDED BY POLICE GUNFIRE.

ALL OF THEM WERE CHARGED WITH THE ATTEMPTED MURDER OF THE POLICE.

LATER THAT MORNING, ILLINOIS STATE'S ATTORNEY, EDWARD HANRAHAN, HELD A PRESS CONFERENCE WHERE HE TOLD A STORY VERY DIFFERENT FROM WHAT HAPPENED.

ACCORDING TO HANRAHAN, HAMPTON AND THE OTHER PANTHERS IN THE APARTMENT OPENED FIRE ON THE POLICE.

THE TRUTH IS THAT HAMPTON DIDN'T FIRE A SINGLE SHOT THAT MORNING. HE NEVER EVEN WOKE UP.

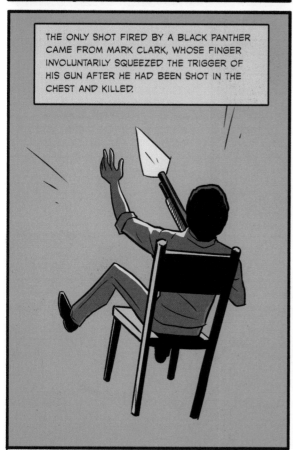

THE ONLY SHOT FIRED BY A BLACK PANTHER CAME FROM MARK CLARK, WHOSE FINGER INVOLUNTARILY SQUEEZED THE TRIGGER OF HIS GUN AFTER HE HAD BEEN SHOT IN THE CHEST AND KILLED.

THE POLICE OFFICERS WHO CARRIED OUT THE RAID WERE IN PLAIN CLOTHES AND ARMED WITH A MACHINE GUN.

THE POLICE NEVER IDENTIFIED THEMSELVES AS COPS.

THEY FIRED NEARLY A HUNDRED ROUNDS INTO THE APARTMENT.

THE POLICE FAILED TO SECURE THE SCENE OF THE KILLING, AND FEARING AN IMPENDING COVER-UP BY THE POLICE, THE BLACK PANTHERS CONDUCTED TOURS OF THE APARTMENT SO THAT MEMBERS OF THE COMMUNITY AND JOURNALISTS COULD GET A BETTER SENSE OF WHAT REALLY HAPPENED.

IT WAS CLEAR THAT ALL THE SHOTS FIRED WERE GOING INTO THE APARTMENT--COMING FROM POLICE GUNS.

THOUGH HANRAHAN STUCK TO HIS STORY, IT BECAME INCREASINGLY CLEAR THAT HIS ACCOUNT WAS A LIE. THERE WAS MORE TO THE RAID--AND THE KILLINGS-- THAN THE STATE'S ATTORNEY WAS LETTING ON.

ONE THING THAT COULD NOT BE EXPLAINED WAS WHY HAMPTON NEVER WOKE UP, EVEN WITH THE POLICE FIRING MACHINE GUNS INTO THE APARTMENT.

EVIDENCE INDICATES THAT HAMPTON HAD BEEN DRUGGED EARLIER IN THE NIGHT, RENDERING HIM UNCONSCIOUS AS THE POLICE RAIDED HIS HOME.

OVER TIME, THE TRUTH ABOUT HAMPTON'S DEATH WOULD BE REVEALED.

WILLIAM O'NEAL, CHIEF OF SECURITY FOR THE CHICAGO BLACK PANTHER PARTY AND HAMPTON'S PERSONAL BODYGUARD, WAS IN FACT A PAID FBI INFORMANT.

O'NEAL HAD BEEN BUSTED FOR CAR THEFT AND VIOLATING PAROLE WHEN HE WAS APPROACHED BY THE FBI ABOUT INFILTRATING THE PANTHERS.

ALTHOUGH IT HAS NEVER BEEN PROVEN, IT IS HIGHLY LIKELY THAT O'NEAL DRUGGED HAMPTON'S FOOD THE NIGHT OF THE RAID.

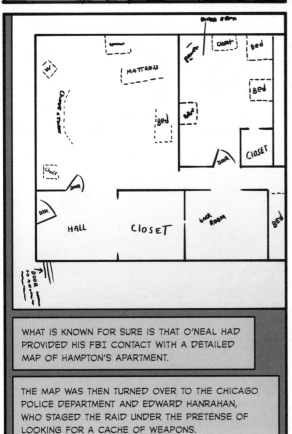

WHAT IS KNOWN FOR SURE IS THAT O'NEAL HAD PROVIDED HIS FBI CONTACT WITH A DETAILED MAP OF HAMPTON'S APARTMENT.

THE MAP WAS THEN TURNED OVER TO THE CHICAGO POLICE DEPARTMENT AND EDWARD HANRAHAN, WHO STAGED THE RAID UNDER THE PRETENSE OF LOOKING FOR A CACHE OF WEAPONS.

FOR PROVIDING CRUCIAL INFORMATION USED IN THE RAID THAT KILLED HAMPTON AND CLARK, WILLIAM O'NEAL WAS PAID A $300 BONUS BY THE FBI.

ON DECEMBER 8, 1969--FOUR DAYS AFTER THE MURDERS OF CLARK AND HAMPTON IN CHICAGO--THE LAPD LAUNCHED A MAJOR OFFENSIVE AGAINST THE BLACK PANTHER PARTY IN LOS ANGELES.

AT 5:00 A.M., POLICE SIMULTANEOUSLY EXECUTED THREE RAIDS--ONE AT THE HOME OF GERONIMO PRATT, THE SECOND AT THE TOURE COMMUNITY CENTER RUN BY THE PANTHERS, AND THE THIRD AT THE PARTY HEADQUARTERS ON 41ST AND CENTRAL.

THE RAID AT 41ST AND CENTRAL STARTED OUT WITH 75 HEAVILY ARMED POLICE OFFICERS--THE FIRST-EVER USE OF A SPECIAL WEAPONS AND TACTICS (SWAT) TEAM.

HAVING ALREADY CLASHED WITH THE POLICE, THE PANTHERS WERE PREPARED TO TAKE A STAND. UNDER THE DIRECTION OF GERONIMO PRATT, THE HEADQUARTERS HAD BEEN FORTIFIED TO DEFEND AGAINST A POTENTIAL RAID, AND IT WAS HEAVILY ARMED.

AS MORE POLICE OFFICERS ARRIVED ON THE SCENE, AND WITH TELEVISION NEWS CAMERAS WATCHING, THE L.A. STREET CORNER OF 41ST AND CENTRAL TURNED INTO A WAR ZONE.

OUTSIDE, ON THE STREET, THE POLICE LAUNCHED TEAR GAS AND FIRED OVER 5,000 ROUNDS OF AMMUNITION.

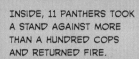

INSIDE, 11 PANTHERS TOOK A STAND AGAINST MORE THAN A HUNDRED COPS AND RETURNED FIRE.

AFTER MORE THAN FOUR HOURS, WOUNDED, OUTGUNNED, AND RUNNING OUT OF BULLETS, THE PANTHERS SURRENDERED.

JUST BEFORE 10:00 A.M., RENEE "PEACHES" MOORE EMERGED FROM THE BULLET-RIDDLED HEADQUARTERS WAVING A WHITE FLAG. AT 19 YEARS OLD, MOORE WAS ONE OF SEVEN TEENAGERS INVOLVED IN THE BATTLE.

THE L.A. BLACK PANTHERS HAD PUT UP A GOOD FIGHT AND, SHORT OF GIVING THEIR LIVES, HAD DONE ALL THEY COULD DO. BUT IN THE END, THEY COULDN'T STAND UP TO THE MASSIVE POWER OF LAW ENFORCEMENT.

THE SHOOT—OUT BETWEEN THE L.A. PANTHERS AND THE POLICE MARKED THE END OF A VERY VIOLENT AND DEADLY YEAR FOR THE BLACK PANTHER PARTY.

John Huggins   Alprentice

MORE THAN 20 RAIDS HAPPENED IN CITIES ACROSS AMERICA IN 1969 AS LAW ENFORCEMENT SOUGHT TO DESTROY THE BLACK PANTHER PARTY. DOZENS OF MEMBERS WERE ARRESTED AND AWAITING TRIAL ACROSS THE COUNTRY. AS MANY AS 11 PANTHERS WERE KILLED BY THE POLICE OR BY PROVOCATEURS WORKING FOR THE FBI.

Angela Davis

ONE OF THE LEADING ACTIVISTS OF THE 1960s, ANGELA DAVIS FIRST BECAME INVOLVED WITH THE BLACK PANTHER PARTY OF LOS ANGELES--ONE OF THE BLACK POWER ORGANIZATIONS INSPIRED BY THE LCFO BUT NOT AFFILIATED WITH THE OAKLAND-BASED PANTHERS.

BORN IN ALABAMA IN 1944, DAVIS BECAME A CONTROVERSIAL FIGURE IN THE 1960s AS A MEMBER OF THE COMMUNIST PARTY. WHILE SHE WAS WORKING AS AN ASSISTANT PROFESSOR AT UCLA, GOVERNOR RONALD REAGAN CONVINCED THE UNIVERSITY'S BOARD OF REGENTS TO FIRE DAVIS IN 1969 FOR HER POLITICAL BELIEFS.

AS THE OAKLAND-BASED PANTHERS FIRST LOOKED TO EXPAND TO L.A., TENSION DEVELOPED BETWEEN THE PANTHERS IN THE TWO CITIES. WITH THOSE CONFLICTS RESOLVED IN 1968, DAVIS JOINED THE L.A. CHAPTER OF THE BLACK PANTHER PARTY FOR SELF-DEFENSE, AND THE OTHER PANTHER PARTY DISBANDED.

DEVASTATED BY THE MURDER OF JOHN HUGGINS AND DISAPPOINTED BY THE PURGES MEANT TO WEED OUT PROVOCATEURS IN THE PARTY, DAVIS STEPPED AWAY FROM THE DAY-TO-DAY ACTIVITY OF THE PANTHERS, THOUGH HER INVOLVEMENT AND INFLUENCE CONTINUED.

IN JUNE OF 1970, DAVIS BECAME INVOLVED WITH THE SOLEDAD BROTHERS DEFENSE COMMITTEE, WHICH WAS WORKING WITH JAILED PANTHER GEORGE JACKSON AND FELLOW INMATES JOHN CLUTCHETTE AND FLEETA DRUMGO, WHO WERE ACCUSED OF KILLING A PRISON GUARD.

THE FOLLOWING MONTH, AT THE MARIN COUNTY COURTHOUSE IN CALIFORNIA, JACKSON'S BROTHER JONATHAN TOOK JUDGE HAROLD HALEY HOSTAGE IN A FAILED ATTEMPT TO GET GEORGE OUT OF PRISON. BOTH JONATHAN JACKSON AND HALEY WERE KILLED. THE GUN USED BY JACKSON HAD BELONGED TO ANGELA DAVIS, WHO WAS CHARGED WITH CONSPIRACY, KIDNAPPING, AND MURDER IN THE DEATH OF HALEY.

WITH A WARRANT ISSUED FOR HER ARREST, DAVIS WENT UNDERGROUND. THE FBI PLACED HER ON THE TEN MOST WANTED FUGITIVES LIST, AND ON OCTOBER 13, 1970, SHE WAS ARRESTED IN NEW YORK CITY.

AFTER 16 MONTHS IN JAIL AWAITING HER TRIAL, DAVIS WAS RELEASED ON BAIL IN 1972. HER TRIAL FOLLOWED SHORTLY, AND ON JUNE 4, 1972, SHE WAS FOUND NOT GUILTY OF THE CHARGES RELATED TO THE DEATH OF HAROLD HALEY.

George Jackson

BORN ON SEPTEMBER 23, 1941, IN CHICAGO, GEORGE JACKSON WAS SENTENCED TO ONE YEAR TO LIFE FOR A GAS STATION ROBBERY--HE STOLE JUST $70. HE WAS 19 AT THE TIME.

WHILE LOCKED UP IN SOLEDAD STATE PRISON, JACKSON BECAME POLITICIZED AND FOUNDED THE BLACK GUERRILLA FAMILY, AN ORGANIZATION DETERMINED TO EDUCATE BLACK PRISONERS AND TURN THEM INTO REVOLUTIONARIES.

JACKSON BEGAN COMMUNICATING WITH HUEY NEWTON WHILE NEWTON WAS IN PRISON FOR THE KILLING OF JOHN FREY, WHICH LED TO GEORGE FORMING THE FIRST BRANCH OF THE PANTHERS IN PRISON.

IN 1970, AFTER BEING CHARGED WITH THE DEATH OF A PRISON GUARD, JACKSON AND HIS FELLOW SOLEDAD BROTHERS FACED THE DEATH PENALTY.

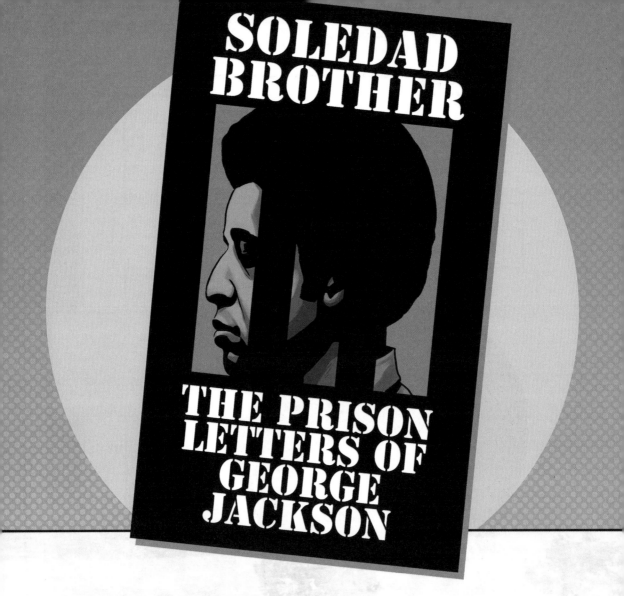

TO PUBLICIZE THE SOLEDAD BROTHERS' CASE, RAISE MONEY FOR THEIR DEFENSE, AND SHED LIGHT ON THE CONDITIONS FACED BY PRISONERS, JACKSON'S LAWYER, FAY STENDER, ARRANGED TO PUBLISH A SERIES OF LETTERS WRITTEN BY JACKSON, *SOLEDAD BROTHER: THE PRISON LETTERS OF GEORGE JACKSON.*

FOUNDER OF THE SOLEDAD BROTHERS DEFENSE COMMITTEE, STENDER WAS A RADICAL LEFTIST LAWYER WHO WORKED WITH NEWTON'S LAWYER, CHARLES GARRY. STENDER WAS ONE OF THE PEOPLE THROUGH WHOM JACKSON AND NEWTON COMMUNICATED WHILE BOTH WERE IMPRISONED.

SEVERAL MONTHS BEFORE THE RELEASE OF *SOLEDAD BROTHER* IN 1970, THE INCIDENT AT THE MARIN COUNTY COURTHOUSE RESULTING IN THE DEATHS OF JONATHAN JACKSON AND HAROLD HALEY OCCURRED. THIS BROUGHT MORE ATTENTION TO THE CASE OF GEORGE JACKSON, AND WHEN *SOLEDAD BROTHER* WAS RELEASED, IT WAS AN INSTANT HIT.

SOLEDAD BROTHER CONTAINED SEVERAL LOVE LETTERS WRITTEN TO ANGELA DAVIS. ON JULY 8, 1971, ANGELA AND GEORGE MET IN PERSON FOR THE FIRST TIME TO DISCUSS HER CASE AND THE POSSIBILITY THAT HE MIGHT BE CALLED AS A WITNESS. SHORTLY AFTER THAT MEETING, ANGELA SENT GEORGE LETTERS EXPRESSING HER LOVE FOR HIM.

ON AUGUST 21, 1971, GEORGE WAS KILLED IN A FAILED ATTEMPT TO ESCAPE FROM SAN QUENTIN STATE PRISON. AFTER GEORGE'S DEATH, ANGELA'S LOVE LETTERS WERE FOUND IN HIS CELL AND USED TO ESTABLISH A MOTIVE FOR HER ALLEGED INVOLVEMENT IN JONATHAN'S ATTEMPT TO FREE HIS BROTHER.

GEORGE'S FUNERAL WAS HELD AT ST. AUGUSTINE'S IN OAKLAND, WHERE HE WAS HONORED AND EULOGIZED AS A FALLEN HERO—A MARTYR TO THE CAUSE OF BLACK LIBERATION. LESS THAN A YEAR LATER, THE TWO REMAINING SOLEDAD BROTHERS—JOHN CLUTCHETTE AND FLEETA DRUMGO—WERE ACQUITTED OF MURDER CHARGES.

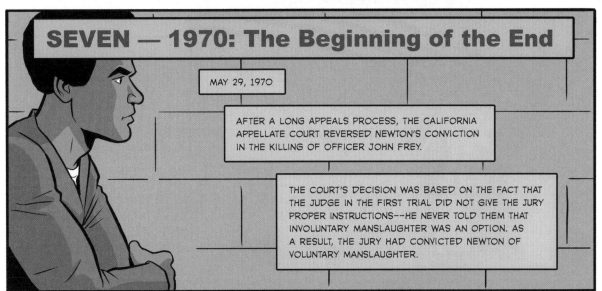

SEVEN — 1970: The Beginning of the End

MAY 29, 1970

AFTER A LONG APPEALS PROCESS, THE CALIFORNIA APPELLATE COURT REVERSED NEWTON'S CONVICTION IN THE KILLING OF OFFICER JOHN FREY.

THE COURT'S DECISION WAS BASED ON THE FACT THAT THE JUDGE IN THE FIRST TRIAL DID NOT GIVE THE JURY PROPER INSTRUCTIONS--HE NEVER TOLD THEM THAT INVOLUNTARY MANSLAUGHTER WAS AN OPTION. AS A RESULT, THE JURY HAD CONVICTED NEWTON OF VOLUNTARY MANSLAUGHTER.

WITH GERONIMO PRATT AND HIS CHILDHOOD FRIEND DAVID HILLIARD AT HIS SIDE, NEWTON WAS RELEASED ON BAIL ON AUGUST 5, 1970. HE HAD BEEN IN PRISON FOR ALMOST THREE YEARS--MORE THAN HALF THE TIME THE BLACK PANTHERS HAD BEEN IN EXISTENCE.

OUTSIDE THE ALAMEDA COUNTY COURTHOUSE, A CROWD OF NEARLY 10,000 HAD GATHERED TO CELEBRATE NEWTON'S RELEASE.

NEWTON WAS GREETED BY THE ENORMOUS CHEERING CROWD. WHILE IN PRISON, HE HAD BECOME A SYMBOL OF SO MANY DIFFERENT IMPORTANT CAUSES THAT WHEN HE WALKED OUT OF THE COURTHOUSE, HE WAS ALREADY A LIVING LEGEND.

NEWTON'S INCARCERATION HAD BEEN ONE OF THE RALLYING POINTS FOR THE BLACK PANTHERS, BRINGING INTERNATIONAL ATTENTION TO THE PARTY AND ITS CAUSE.

FOR MEMBERS OF THE PARTY, AND FOR SUPPORTERS OF THE PANTHERS, THE RELEASE OF NEWTON HAD BEEN A MAJOR VICTORY.

IT WAS ALSO A VICTORY FOR THE ANTI-WAR MOVEMENT, AND FOR ALL THE OTHER RADICAL, FAR-LEFT CAUSES THAT HAD STOOD IN SOLIDARITY WITH THE PANTHERS. HIS RELEASE SEEMED LIKE A VICTORY AGAINST AN OPPRESSIVE GOVERNMENT CRACKING DOWN ON VOCAL DISSIDENTS DEMANDING CHANGE, EQUALITY, AND AN END TO WAR.

WITH SEALE STILL IN PRISON WITH THE NEW HAVEN PANTHERS AND CLEAVER IN ALGERIA, NEWTON RECLAIMED HIS ROLE AS LEADER OF THE PARTY, TAKING BACK THE REINS FROM HIS BEST FRIEND, DAVID HILLIARD.

THOUGH HE WAS OUT ON BAIL, NEWTON'S PROBLEMS WERE NOT OVER. HE WOULD STILL FACE TWO MORE TRIALS IN THE KILLING OF JOHN FREY—NOW FOR INVOLUNTARY MANSLAUGHTER. THE SECOND TRIAL WOULD END IN A HUNG JURY, AND THE THIRD TRIAL WOULD END IN A DISMISSAL. NEWTON WAS FINALLY FREE.

SURVIVAL PENDING REVOLUTION

AFTER HIS RELEASE FROM PRISON, NEWTON BEGAN TO TAKE THE BLACK PANTHER PARTY IN A NEW DIRECTION THAT DOWNPLAYED GUNS AND REVOLUTION--AND EMPHASIZED HELPING THE COMMUNITY. BUILDING ON THE SUCCESS OF THE FREE BREAKFAST FOR SCHOOL CHILDREN PROGRAM, THE PANTHERS LAUNCHED THEIR SURVIVAL PROGRAMS.

WE RECOGNIZED THAT IN ORDER TO BRING THE PEOPLE TO THE LEVEL OF CONSCIOUSNESS WHERE THEY WOULD SEIZE THE TIME, IT WOULD BE NECESSARY TO SERVE THEIR INTERESTS IN SURVIVAL BY DEVELOPING PROGRAMS WHICH WOULD HELP THEM MEET THEIR DAILY NEEDS.

NOW WE NOT ONLY HAVE A BREAKFAST PROGRAM FOR SCHOOLCHILDREN, WE HAVE CLOTHING PROGRAMS, WE HAVE HEALTH CLINICS WHICH PROVIDE FREE MEDICAL AND DENTAL SERVICES, WE HAVE PROGRAMS FOR PRISONERS AND THEIR FAMILIES, AND WE ARE OPENING CLOTHING AND SHOE FACTORIES TO PROVIDE FOR MORE OF THE NEEDS OF THE COMMUNITY.

ALL THESE PROGRAMS SATISFY THE DEEP NEEDS OF THE COMMUNITY BUT THEY ARE NOT SOLUTIONS TO OUR PROBLEMS. THAT IS WHY WE CALL THEM SURVIVAL PROGRAMS, MEANING SURVIVAL PENDING REVOLUTION.

WE SAY THAT THE SURVIVAL PROGRAM OF THE BLACK PANTHER PARTY IS LIKE THE SURVIVAL KIT OF A SAILOR STRANDED ON A RAFT. IT HELPS HIM TO SUSTAIN HIMSELF UNTIL HE CAN GET COMPLETELY OUT OF THAT SITUATION.

SO THE SURVIVAL PROGRAMS ARE NOT ANSWERS OR SOLUTIONS, BUT THEY WILL HELP US TO ORGANIZE THE COMMUNITY AROUND A TRUE ANALYSIS AND UNDERSTANDING OF THEIR SITUATION.

WHEN CONSCIOUSNESS AND UNDERSTANDING IS RAISED TO A HIGH LEVEL THEN THE COMMUNITY WILL SEIZE THE TIME AND DELIVER THEMSELVES FROM THE BOOT OF THEIR OPPRESSORS.

DIFFERENT CHAPTERS OF THE PARTY IMPLEMENTED DIFFERENT SURVIVAL PROGRAMS, PROVIDING A WIDE RANGE OF SERVICES AND RESOURCES TO THEIR COMMUNITIES.

SENIORS AGAINST A FEARFUL ENVIRONMENT (SAFE) PROVIDED ELDERLY MEMBERS OF THE COMMUNITY WITH ESCORTS AS THEY RAN ERRANDS.

THE FREE BUSING TO PRISONS PROGRAM PROVIDED TRANSPORTATION SERVICES TO THE FAMILIES OF INCARCERATED PEOPLE, ALLOWING VISITATION ACCESS.

OTHER PROGRAMS OFFERED FREE CLOTHING AND SHOES.

THE FREE FOOD PROGRAM GAVE OUT 10,000 BAGS OF FREE GROCERIES IN OAKLAND IN 1972.

ALL TOLD, NEARLY 60 DIFFERENT SURVIVAL PROGRAMS WERE LAUNCHED BY BLACK PANTHER CHAPTERS ALL OVER THE COUNTRY.

PEOPLE'S
PEOPLE'S
PEOPLE'S
PEOPLE'S
LE'S
PEOPLE'S FREE FOOD PROGRAM
PEOPLE'S FREE FOOD PROGRAM
OOD RAM

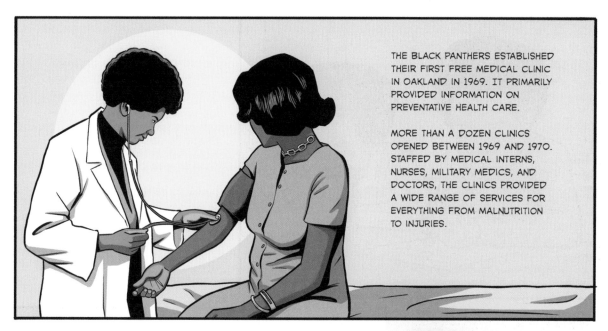

THE BLACK PANTHERS ESTABLISHED THEIR FIRST FREE MEDICAL CLINIC IN OAKLAND IN 1969. IT PRIMARILY PROVIDED INFORMATION ON PREVENTATIVE HEALTH CARE.

MORE THAN A DOZEN CLINICS OPENED BETWEEN 1969 AND 1970. STAFFED BY MEDICAL INTERNS, NURSES, MILITARY MEDICS, AND DOCTORS, THE CLINICS PROVIDED A WIDE RANGE OF SERVICES FOR EVERYTHING FROM MALNUTRITION TO INJURIES.

IN 1971, THE PANTHERS BEGAN A NATIONAL TESTING PROGRAM FOR SICKLE CELL ANEMIA, A DISEASE THAT AFFECTED MOSTLY BLACK AMERICANS. DESPITE THE FACT THAT IT WAS AN EPIDEMIC IN THE U.S., SICKLE CELL ANEMIA WAS NOT A PRIORITY OF THE MAINSTREAM MEDICAL WORLD.

THE BLACK PANTHER PARTY'S SICKLE CELL ANEMIA PROJECT PROVIDED TESTING AND COUNSELING FOR MORE THAN A MILLION PATIENTS AND BROUGHT NATIONAL ATTENTION TO THE DISEASE.

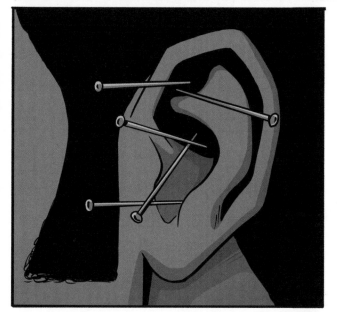

IN 1972, A CONTINGENT OF PANTHERS VISITED CHINA. DR. TOLBERT SMALL, THE PANTHERS' MEDICAL ADVISER, LEARNED TO PERFORM ACUPUNCTURE ON THAT TRIP, AND HE WAS CRUCIAL IN INTRODUCING THE PRACTICE TO POOR, URBAN COMMUNITIES IN THE U.S.

THE PANTHERS BECAME EARLY ADOPTERS AND ADVOCATES OF PRACTICING FIVE-POINT EAR ACUPUNCTURE, WHICH CAN BE USED AS A TREATMENT FOR DRUG ADDICTION.

THE BLACK PANTHER PARTY HAD DEVELOPED ITS FIRST EDUCATIONAL PROGRAM IN 1969 WITH THEIR LIBERATION SCHOOLS.

THE INTERCOMMUNAL YOUTH INSTITUTE GREW OUT OF THE LIBERATION SCHOOLS IN 1971 AND WAS RENAMED THE OAKLAND COMMUNITY SCHOOL (OCS) IN 1973. THE OCS WAS A PRIVATE SCHOOL OPERATED BY EDUCATIONAL OPPORTUNITIES CORPORATION, THE PANTHERS' NONPROFIT AND THE LAST OF THE PARTY'S EDUCATION INITIATIVES.

ERICKA HUGGINS RAN THE OCS FROM 1973 TO 1981. WITH A STAFF OF ACCREDITED TEACHERS AND A TEAM OF AIDES AND VOLUNTEERS, THE OCS OFFERED A FULL RANGE OF COURSES TO ITS 120 STUDENTS. THE STUDENTS, RANGING IN AGE FROM 2 TO 11, WERE SERVED THREE MEALS A DAY.

OF ALL THE SURVIVAL PROGRAMS LAUNCHED BY THE PANTHERS IN THE 1970s, THE OCS WAS THE MOST SUCCESSFUL. BY THE TIME THE OCS CLOSED IN 1982, HUNDREDS OF STUDENTS HAD GONE THROUGH THE PROGRAM.

DESPITE THE IMPLEMENTATION OF THE SURVIVAL PROGRAMS AS AN EFFORT TO REDEFINE AND REVITALIZE THE BLACK PANTHERS, THE PARTY WAS FALLING APART.

BETWEEN 1966, WHEN THE BLACK PANTHERS WERE FOUNDED, AND 1970, THE WORLD, THE POLITICAL LANDSCAPE, AND THE PARTY ITSELF HAD CHANGED DRASTICALLY. AND, OF COURSE, HUEY NEWTON HIMSELF HAD CHANGED.

AFTER HIS RELEASE FROM PRISON, NEWTON'S BEHAVIOR BECAME INCREASINGLY ERRATIC AND PARANOID, FUELED BY A DEADLY COMBINATION OF SUBSTANCE ABUSE AND UNRELENTING COINTELPRO ACTIONS AGAINST THE PANTHERS.

ON THE ORDERS OF NEWTON, HILLIARD EXPELLED GERONIMO PRATT FROM THE PANTHERS BECAUSE PRATT HAD GONE UNDERGROUND AND WAS WORKING WITH THE BLACK LIBERATION ARMY--A MORE RADICAL, UNAFFILIATED OFFSHOOT OF THE PANTHERS.

SHORTLY AFTER, THE PANTHER 21 IN NEW YORK WERE ALSO EXPELLED BY NEWTON, BECAUSE THEY, TOO, WERE CALLING FOR ARMED REVOLUTION.

NEWTON'S DECISION TO EXPEL SUCH HIGH-PROFILE MEMBERS SERVED TO CREATE A RIFT IN AN ORGANIZATION THAT WAS ALREADY FRACTURED.

TWO WEEKS LATER, NEWTON AND CLEAVER APPEARED ON A LIVE TELEVISION NEWS BROADCAST. FROM ALGERIA, CLEAVER BLASTED HILLIARD, WHO HE BLAMED FOR THE EXPULSION OF GERONIMO PRATT AND THE PANTHER 21.

CLEAVER'S COMMENTS MADE PUBLIC THE INTERNAL CONFLICTS WITHIN THE PARTY. NEWTON TOOK CLEAVER'S ATTACK ON HILLIARD PERSONALLY, AS HILLIARD HAD BEEN FOLLOWING NEWTON'S ORDERS.

EIGHT — 1971–1988: Death of the Panthers

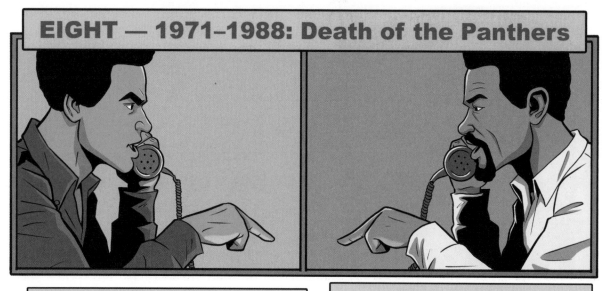

AFTER THE BROADCAST, NEWTON CALLED CLEAVER IN ALGERIA--A CONVERSATION THAT CLEAVER RECORDED. IN A TENSE, VOLATILE EXCHANGE, NEWTON CALLED CLEAVER A COWARD AND BLAMED HIM FOR THE DEATH OF LIL' BOBBY HUTTON.

CLEAVER RESPONDED BY INSULTING NEWTON AND MAKING THREATS. THE CONVERSATION ENDED WITH NEWTON EXPELLING CLEAVER AND HIS ALGERIAN CADRE OF PANTHERS.

THIS WAS THE BEGINNING OF A RIFT THAT WOULD HELP TO DESTROY THE BLACK PANTHERS.

IDEOLOGICAL DIFFERENCES AND TENSIONS EXISTED IN THE BLACK PANTHER PARTY FROM THE BEGINNING. OVER TIME, THESE DIFFERENCES BECAME MORE PRONOUNCED.

STUCK IN PRISON FROM 1967 TO 1970, HUEY NEWTON FELT THAT LIBERATION WOULD ONLY COME THROUGH REVOLUTION, AND THAT THE WORKING CLASS WHO SHOULD LEAD THE REVOLUTION NEEDED TO BE READY FOR THE FIGHT TO COME. BUT NEWTON DID NOT BELIEVE THE PEOPLE WERE READY YET.

LIVING IN EXILE IN ALGERIA, ELDRIDGE CLEAVER BELIEVED THAT THE REVOLUTION NEEDED TO HAPPEN IMMEDIATELY, AND THAT IT COULD BE FOUGHT BY THE LUMPENPROLETARIAT--THE UNEMPLOYED, CRIMINALS, AND THE UNDERCLASS OF SOCIETY. CLEAVER THOUGHT NEWTON'S SURVIVAL PROGRAMS WERE A WASTE OF TIME.

THE DIFFERING IDEOLOGIES OF NEWTON AND CLEAVER ESSENTIALLY CREATED TWO FACTIONS WITHIN THE PARTY. COMPLICATING MATTERS WAS THE FBI'S COUNTERINTELLIGENCE PROGRAM, WHICH EFFECTIVELY PLAYED BOTH SIDES AGAINST EACH OTHER IN AN EFFORT TO TEAR THE PANTHERS APART.

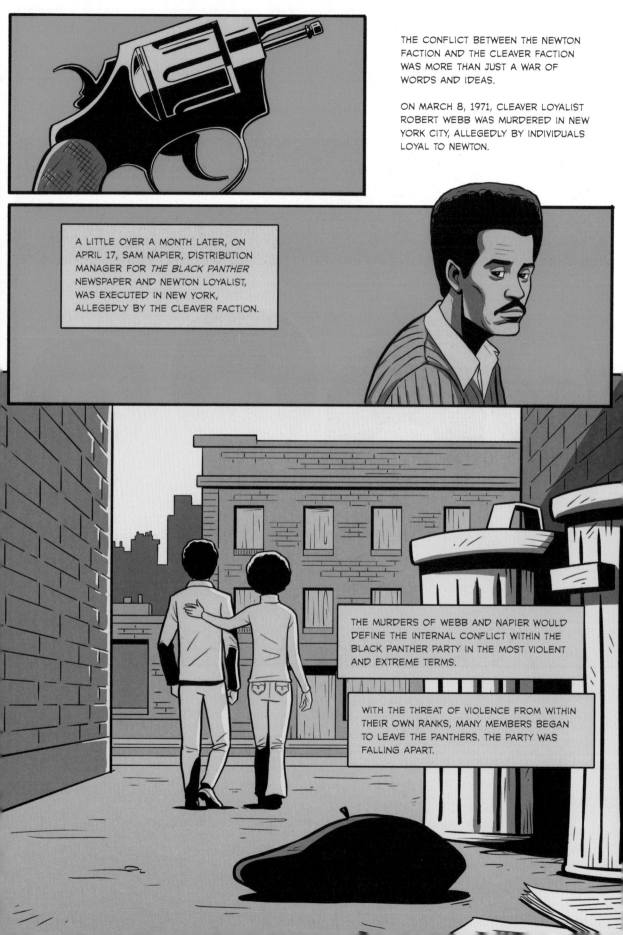

THE CONFLICT BETWEEN THE NEWTON FACTION AND THE CLEAVER FACTION WAS MORE THAN JUST A WAR OF WORDS AND IDEAS.

ON MARCH 8, 1971, CLEAVER LOYALIST ROBERT WEBB WAS MURDERED IN NEW YORK CITY, ALLEGEDLY BY INDIVIDUALS LOYAL TO NEWTON.

A LITTLE OVER A MONTH LATER, ON APRIL 17, SAM NAPIER, DISTRIBUTION MANAGER FOR *THE BLACK PANTHER* NEWSPAPER AND NEWTON LOYALIST, WAS EXECUTED IN NEW YORK, ALLEGEDLY BY THE CLEAVER FACTION.

THE MURDERS OF WEBB AND NAPIER WOULD DEFINE THE INTERNAL CONFLICT WITHIN THE BLACK PANTHER PARTY IN THE MOST VIOLENT AND EXTREME TERMS.

WITH THE THREAT OF VIOLENCE FROM WITHIN THEIR OWN RANKS, MANY MEMBERS BEGAN TO LEAVE THE PANTHERS. THE PARTY WAS FALLING APART.

WHILE THE RIFT WITHIN THE BLACK PANTHERS MOTIVATED SOME TO LEAVE THE PARTY AND CAUSED OTHERS TO BE EXPELLED, IT DROVE OTHERS TO TAKE A MORE MILITANT STANCE IN LINE WITH CLEAVER'S IDEOLOGY CALLING FOR GUERRILLA WARFARE.

SOME PANTHERS LEFT THE PARTY AND JOINED THE BLACK LIBERATION ARMY (BLA), AN UNDERGROUND GROUP DEDICATED TO THE LIBERATION OF BLACK AMERICANS THROUGH ACTS OF REVOLUTION, CRIME, AND VIOLENCE AGAINST THE GOVERNMENT.

THOUGH THE PANTHERS AND THE BLA WERE ALIGNED IN SOME WAYS, THEY WERE DIFFERENT ORGANIZATIONS. MEMBERS OF THE PANTHERS WHO BELIEVED IN ARMED REVOLUTION OR HAD BEEN EXPELLED FROM THE PARTY MOVED OVER TO THE BLA.

SOME OF THE VIOLENCE ATTRIBUTED TO THE BLACK PANTHERS IN THE 1970s WAS ACTUALLY CONNECTED TO THE BLA. BETWEEN 1970 AND 1980, THE BLA WAS INVOLVED IN NUMEROUS ALLEGED ACTS OF VIOLENCE--INCLUDING THE KILLING OF POLICE OFFICERS.

THE TARGETED INCARCERATION OF PARTY MEMBERS WAS ONE OF THE MOST SUCCESSFUL TACTICS USED TO WEAKEN THE PANTHERS, AND IT WAS ALSO USED AGAINST THE BLA.

IN SOME CASES, CURRENT AND FORMER PANTHERS SPENT DECADES IN PRISON.

GERONIMO PRATT SPENT 27 YEARS IN PRISON FOR A CRIME HE DIDN'T COMMIT.

PANTHER MEMBER EDWARD POINDEXTER WAS CONVICTED OF KILLING A POLICE OFFICER IN 1970 BASED ON QUESTIONABLE EVIDENCE AND HAS BEEN IN PRISON FOR MORE THAN FOUR DECADES.

ALBERT WOODFOX SPENT 45 YEARS IN PRISON—— 43 OF WHICH WERE IN SOLITARY CONFINEMENT.

IN 1977, BLA MEMBER ASSATA SHAKUR WAS CONVICTED OF MURDERING A POLICE OFFICER FOUR YEARS EARLIER. SHE ESCAPED PRISON IN 1979 AND FLED TO CUBA, WHERE SHE WAS GRANTED POLITICAL ASYLUM.

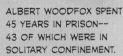

DESPITE REPORTS IDENTIFYING MUMIA ABU-JAMAL AS A MEMBER OF THE BLACK PANTHERS WHEN HE WAS CONVICTED OF KILLING A POLICE OFFICER IN 1982, HE HAD NOT BEEN IN THE PANTHERS SINCE 1970. HE IS CURRENTLY SERVING LIFE IN PRISON.

SUNDIATA ACOLI WAS ONE OF THE PANTHER 21 IN NEW YORK, AND HE WAS A BLA MEMBER WHEN HE WAS CONVICTED OF THE 1973 KILLING OF A POLICE OFFICER. HE IS SERVING A SENTENCE OF LIFE PLUS 30 YEARS.

AS OF 2020, SUNDIATA ACOLI, MUMIA ABU-JAMAL, AND ED POINDEXTER WERE AMONG THE MORE THAN A DOZEN PANTHERS AND FORMER PANTHERS STILL INCARCERATED.

DESPITE THE CONVICTIONS OF THESE PRISONERS AND THE SEVERITY OF THE CHARGES AGAINST THEM, THE CIRCUMSTANCES SURROUNDING MANY OF THESE CASES REMAIN QUESTIONABLE. SOME CASES WERE THE RESULT OF COINTELPRO ACTIONS, AND OFTENTIMES INFORMATION AVAILABLE TO THE PUBLIC ABOUT PRISONERS AND THEIR CONVICTIONS HAS BEEN FILTERED THROUGH COUNTERINTELLIGENCE.

IN ADDITION TO THOSE STILL INCARCERATED, THERE WERE DOZENS OF OTHERS WHO SPENT TIME IN PRISON--OFTEN FOR CRIMES THEY DID NOT COMMIT.

WITH MEMBERSHIP DWINDLING, NEWTON SOUGHT TO RESTRUCTURE THE BLACK PANTHERS AND TAKE THE ORGANIZATION IN A NEW DIRECTION.

IN 1972, THE PANTHERS MADE MOVES TO GET INVOLVED WITH LOCAL POLITICS: BOBBY SEALE RAN FOR MAYOR OF OAKLAND, AND ELAINE BROWN RAN FOR OAKLAND CITY COUNCIL.

NEWTON ISSUED THE ORDER THAT ALL CHAPTERS OF THE PARTY WERE TO CLOSE DOWN AND MEMBERS WERE TO RELOCATE TO OAKLAND, WHICH WOULD BECOME THE SOLE BASE OF OPERATIONS FOR THE BLACK PANTHERS.

THE IDEA WAS TO BUILD A POLITICAL FORCE, STARTING IN OAKLAND, THAT WOULD EVOKE CHANGE FROM WITHIN THE SYSTEM AND THEN SPREAD TO OTHER CITIES.

UNFORTUNATELY, DESPITE MEMBERS FROM ALL OVER THE COUNTRY MOVING TO OAKLAND, THE PLAN DID NOT WORK. NEITHER SEALE NOR BROWN WON THEIR POLITICAL RACES. NEWTON'S PLAN TO BREATHE NEW LIFE INTO THE PANTHERS FAILED, AND WITH ALL OTHER CHAPTERS HAVING SHUT DOWN, THE PARTY CONTINUED TO FALL APART.

MAKE YOUR VOTE COUNT ON APRIL 17TH ELECT TWO DEMOCRATS!

Elect BOBBY SEALE MAYOR OF OAKLAND AND Elect ELAINE BROWN COUNCILWOMAN

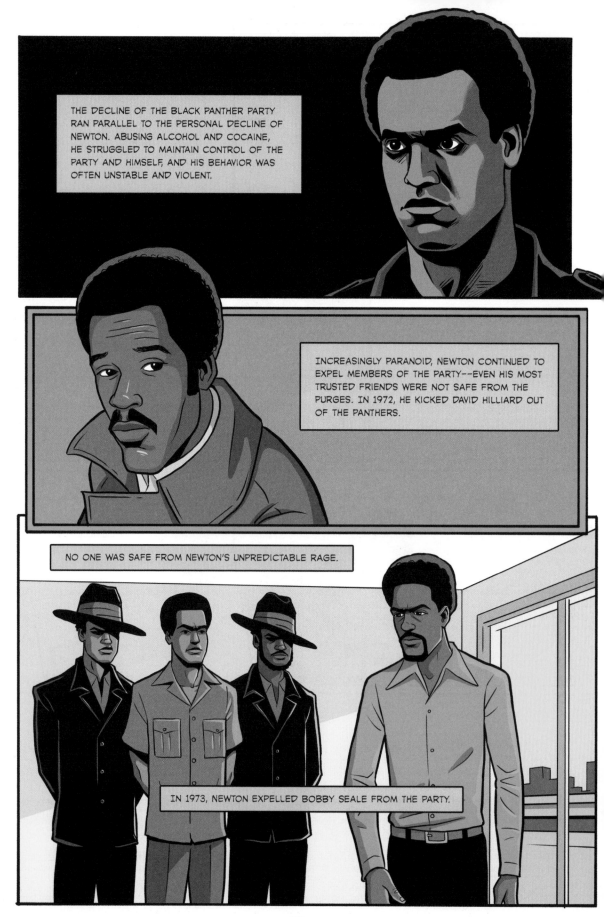

THE DECLINE OF THE BLACK PANTHER PARTY RAN PARALLEL TO THE PERSONAL DECLINE OF NEWTON. ABUSING ALCOHOL AND COCAINE, HE STRUGGLED TO MAINTAIN CONTROL OF THE PARTY AND HIMSELF, AND HIS BEHAVIOR WAS OFTEN UNSTABLE AND VIOLENT.

INCREASINGLY PARANOID, NEWTON CONTINUED TO EXPEL MEMBERS OF THE PARTY—-EVEN HIS MOST TRUSTED FRIENDS WERE NOT SAFE FROM THE PURGES. IN 1972, HE KICKED DAVID HILLIARD OUT OF THE PANTHERS.

NO ONE WAS SAFE FROM NEWTON'S UNPREDICTABLE RAGE.

IN 1973, NEWTON EXPELLED BOBBY SEALE FROM THE PARTY.

SURROUNDING HIMSELF WITH ONLY THE MOST LOYAL OF PARTY MEMBERS, NEWTON LED THE PANTHERS DOWN A DARK PATH OF CRIMINALITY IN OAKLAND. NEWTON AND HIS CREW BEGAN SHAKING DOWN LOCAL GANGSTERS, TAKING MONEY UNDER THE PRETENSE OF USING IT TO FUND THE PARTY.

IN REALITY, NEWTON AND HIS FOLLOWERS WERE TURNING INTO A CRIMINAL ORGANIZATION KNOWN FOR ITS VIOLENCE. RUMORS BEGAN TO CIRCULATE IN THE BAY AREA OF DRUG DEALERS AND PIMPS WHO WERE KILLED BY NEWTON'S GANG OF PANTHERS.

IN 1974, NEWTON WAS ARRESTED ON TWO SEPARATE CHARGES--THE ASSAULT OF PRESTON CALLINS AND THE MURDER OF 17-YEAR-OLD KATHLEEN SMITH. OUT ON BAIL AND AWAITING TRIAL, NEWTON FLED THE COUNTRY, GOING INTO EXILE IN CUBA, WHERE HE WOULD REMAIN UNTIL 1977.

AFTER THE EXPULSION OF SEALE IN 1973, NEWTON APPOINTED ELAINE BROWN CHAIRMAN OF THE CENTRAL COMMITTEE--MAKING HER SECOND IN COMMAND OF THE BLACK PANTHERS.

WHEN NEWTON FLED THE COUNTRY IN 1974, ELAINE TOOK OVER AS LEADER OF THE PARTY, RUNNING THE ENTIRE ORGANIZATION.

ELAINE BROWN LED THE PARTY FROM AUGUST 1974 TO JUNE 1977. SHE DID HER BEST TO SALVAGE WHAT REMAINED OF THE PANTHERS, TAKING THE ORGANIZATION IN A NEW DIRECTION.

ELAINE DEVELOPED STRONG ALLIANCES WITHIN LOCAL POLITICS. SHE BROUGHT THE SUPPORT OF BLACK VOTERS IN OAKLAND TO JERRY BROWN'S RUN FOR GOVERNOR, HELPING HIM WIN. SHE THEN LEVERAGED HER SUPPORT TO GET GOVERNOR BROWN TO APPROVE A $35 MILLION FREEWAY EXTENSION TO OAKLAND, STIMULATING ECONOMIC DEVELOPMENT AND CREATING THOUSANDS OF NEW JOBS.

USING HER CONNECTIONS AND SAVVY, ELAINE HELPED ELECT LIONEL WILSON AS THE FIRST BLACK MAYOR OF OAKLAND. AFTER A PERIOD OF DECLINE CAUSED BY COINTELPRO ACTIONS AND INTER-PARTY CONFLICTS, THE BLACK PANTHERS WERE REINVIGORATED IN OAKLAND.

THE PLAN HAD BEEN TO BUILD THE POLITICAL MACHINERY OF THE PANTHERS INTO SOMETHING THAT COULD HAVE AN EFFECT ON ELECTIONS BEYOND OAKLAND. BUT DESPITE THE PARTY'S EFFECTIVENESS IN BAY AREA POLITICS, IT WAS UNABLE TO GROW BEYOND THE REGION.

IN 1977, NEWTON RETURNED FROM EXILE IN CUBA AND RECLAIMED HIS ROLE AS LEADER OF THE BLACK PANTHERS. AFTER HIS RETURN, ELAINE RESIGNED FROM THE PARTY.

NEWTON RETURNED TO THE U.S. IN 1977 TO FACE CHARGES OF ASSAULT AND MURDER.

AFTER SEVERAL TRIALS, BOTH CASES BEGAN TO UNRAVEL, AND NEWTON WAS ACQUITTED OF BOTH CRIMES--BUT HIS REPUTATION AND THE REPUTATION OF THE PANTHERS WERE DAMAGED.

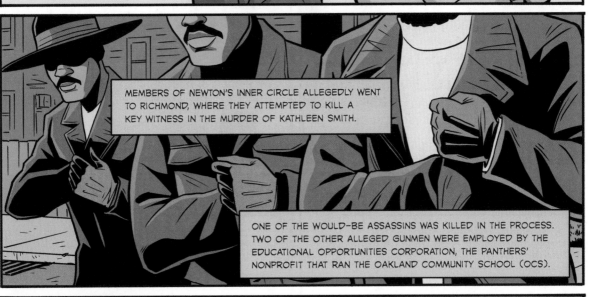

MEMBERS OF NEWTON'S INNER CIRCLE ALLEGEDLY WENT TO RICHMOND, WHERE THEY ATTEMPTED TO KILL A KEY WITNESS IN THE MURDER OF KATHLEEN SMITH.

ONE OF THE WOULD-BE ASSASSINS WAS KILLED IN THE PROCESS. TWO OF THE OTHER ALLEGED GUNMEN WERE EMPLOYED BY THE EDUCATIONAL OPPORTUNITIES CORPORATION, THE PANTHERS' NONPROFIT THAT RAN THE OAKLAND COMMUNITY SCHOOL (OCS).

Gunmen Try to Kill Witness Against Black Panther Leader

OAKLAND, Calif., — Tom Orloff, the deputy prosecutor in a case against Huey P. Newton, said in court yesterday that an

Orloff, said in court yester that the alleged attempt on N Gary's life occurred e Sunday and failed because supposed assassin had gon

MEDIA COVERAGE SURROUNDING THE RICHMOND INCIDENT ONLY SERVED TO WORSEN THE REPUTATION OF THE PARTY AND UNDO THE WORK ELAINE BROWN HAD DONE TO REVITALIZE THE PANTHERS.

crary, testified today that in 1974 she saw Mr. Newton

ters in Berkeley as his address.

IN THE WAKE OF THE RICHMOND INCIDENT, SUPPORTERS AND ALLIES OF THE PARTY BEGAN TO DISTANCE THEMSELVES. FINANCIAL SUPPORT DIMINISHED, AND SOON THE PARTY FACED ANOTHER CRISIS--THERE WAS NOT ENOUGH MONEY TO KEEP IT OPERATIONAL.

FREE HUEY

THE FINANCIAL CRISIS OF THE BLACK PANTHERS HAD A TREMENDOUS IMPACT ON PARTY MEMBERS WHO HAD DEDICATED THEIR LIVES TO KEEPING THE ORGANIZATION AND ITS PROGRAMS RUNNING.

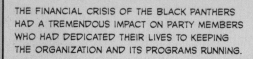

RANK-AND-FILE MEMBERS WORKED DAY AND NIGHT TO KEEP SURVIVAL PROGRAMS AND THE OCS RUNNING, BUT IT PROVED TO BE AN UPHILL BATTLE.

BY 1979, THERE WERE FEWER THAN 60 ACTIVE MEMBERS IN THE PARTY, AND THAT NUMBER DROPPED BELOW 30 IN 1980.

IN 1980, FORMER CALIFORNIA GOVERNOR--AND NEMESIS OF THE BLACK PANTHER PARTY--RONALD REAGAN WAS ELECTED PRESIDENT OF THE UNITED STATES.

REAGAN'S ELECTION WOULD HAVE BEEN A DEVASTATING BLOW TO THE PANTHERS--IF THE PARTY WEREN'T ALREADY CLOSE TO DEATH.

ELDRIDGE CLEAVER BEGAN HIS FIRST OF SEVERAL RELIGIOUS CONVERSIONS IN 1972. HE RETURNED TO THE U.S. IN 1977, AND IN THE 1980s, HE BECAME A CONSERVATIVE REPUBLICAN--THE VERY THING HE ONCE RALLIED AGAINST.

IN 1987, SEALE WROTE A COOKBOOK BEFORE GOING ON TO WRITE A SECOND AUTOBIOGRAPHY IN 1988.

BARBEQUE'N WITH Bobby

RIGHTEOUS, DOWN-HOME BARBEQUE

AS THE PARTY STRUGGLED TO STAY ALIVE, NEWTON WENT ON TO EARN HIS PHD IN SOCIAL PHILOSOPHY FROM UC SANTA CRUZ IN 1980.

MEANWHILE, NEWTON'S SUBSTANCE ABUSE CONTINUED. HE FACED NEW LEGAL PROBLEMS, INCLUDING CHARGES OF POSSESSING A GUN AS AN EX-FELON, AND ALLEGATIONS OF STEALING FUNDS FROM THE OCS AND FALSIFYING RECORDS.

THE FINAL CONTROVERSY SURROUNDING NEWTON PROVED TO BE TOO MUCH. SUPPORT FOR THE OCS—THE PANTHERS' LAST FUNCTIONING PROGRAM—DIED OFF, MAKING IT IMPOSSIBLE TO KEEP THE SCHOOL OPERATING.

OAKLAND COMMUNITY SCHOOL

IN 1982, THE OCS CLOSED, THE LAST REMAINING MEMBERS OF THE BLACK PANTHERS LEFT THE ORGANIZATION, AND THE PARTY DIED.

AFTER THE DEATH OF THE PANTHER PARTY, NEWTON CONTINUED A DOWNWARD SPIRAL INTO CRACK COCAINE ADDICTION. HE HAD BEEN IN AND OUT OF PRISON AGAIN, AND ON THE STREETS OF OAKLAND, HE HAD A REPUTATION FOR ROBBING CRACK DEALERS.

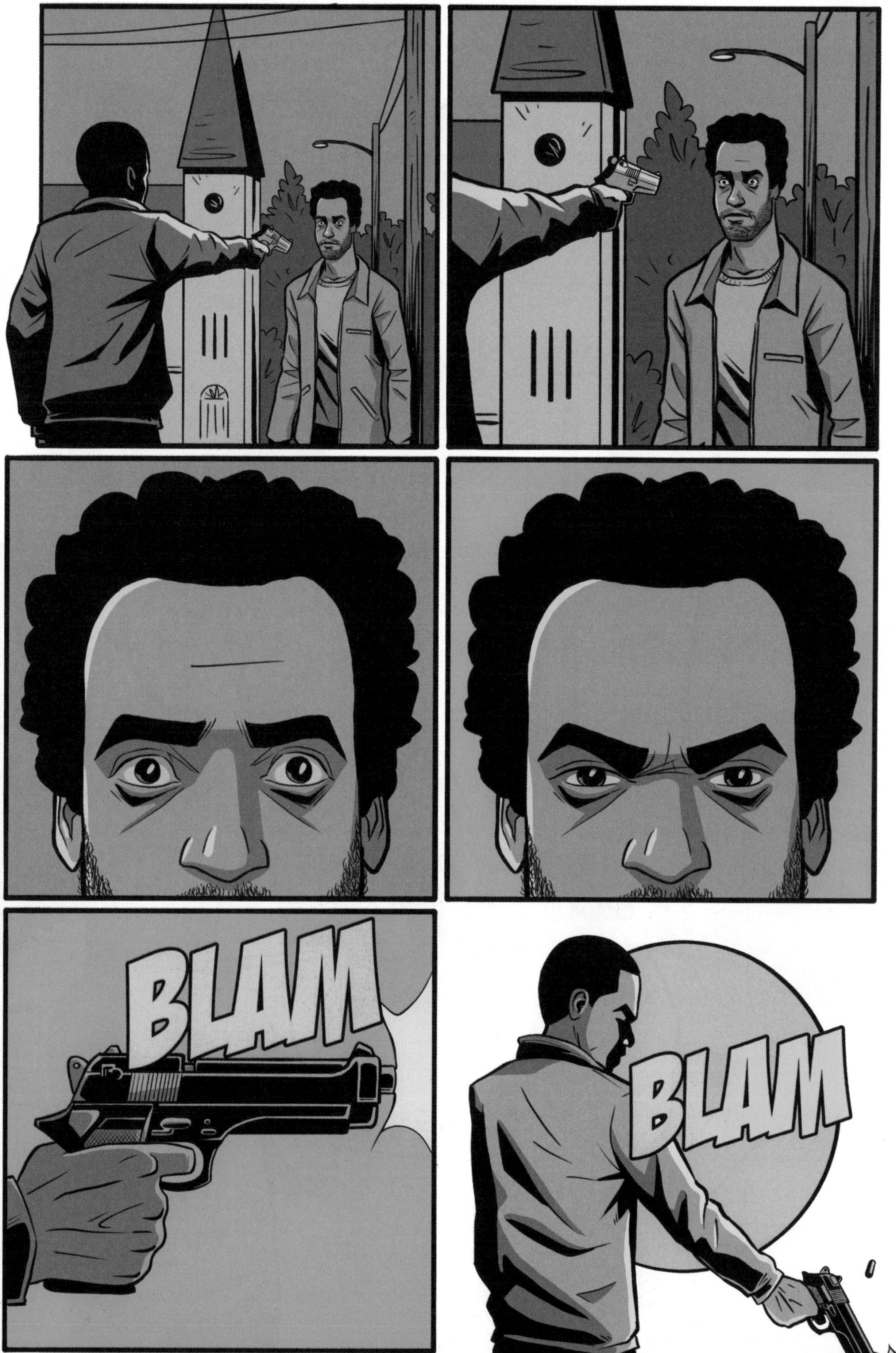
BLAM
BLAM

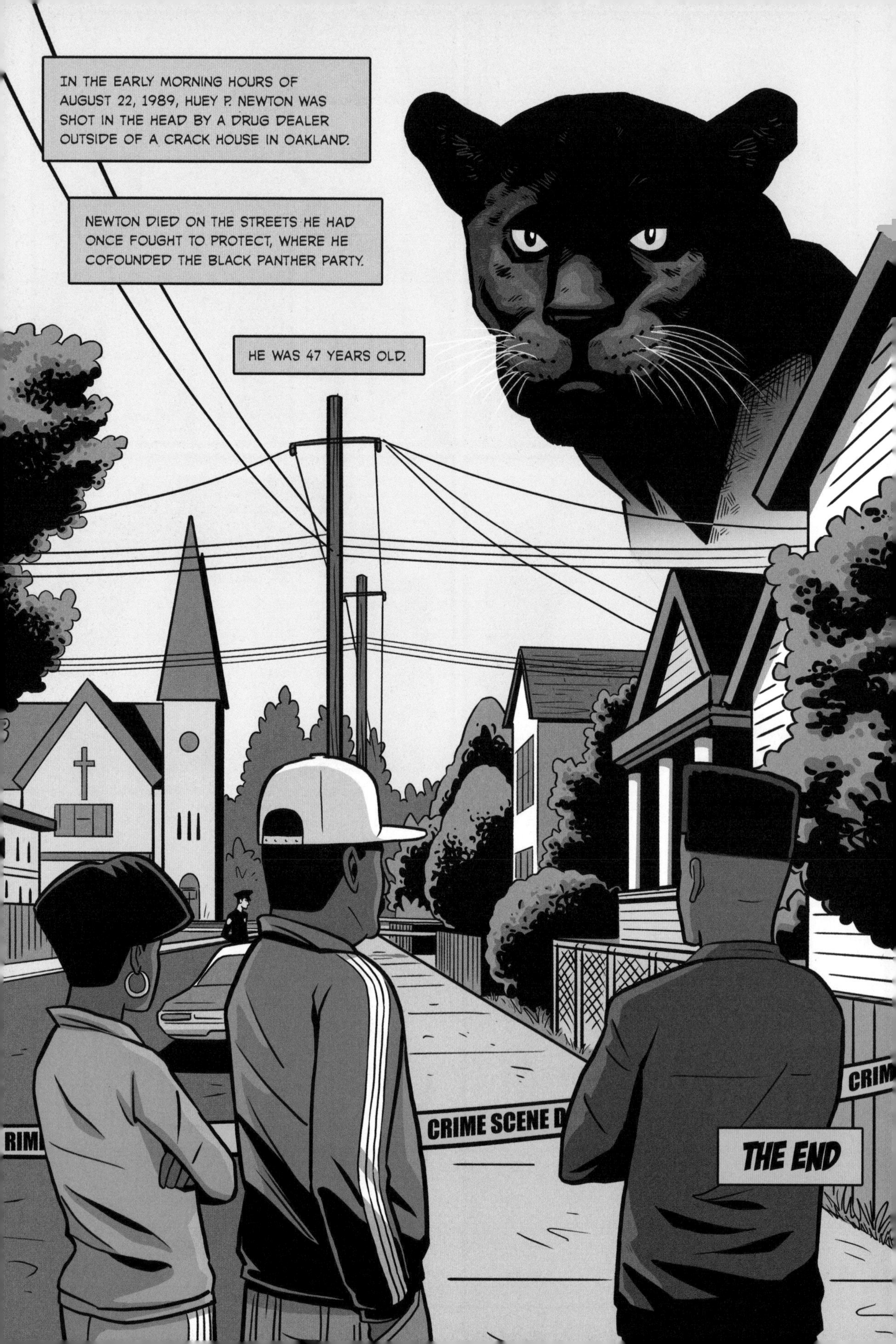
IN THE EARLY MORNING HOURS OF AUGUST 22, 1989, HUEY P. NEWTON WAS SHOT IN THE HEAD BY A DRUG DEALER OUTSIDE OF A CRACK HOUSE IN OAKLAND.
NEWTON DIED ON THE STREETS HE HAD ONCE FOUGHT TO PROTECT, WHERE HE COFOUNDED THE BLACK PANTHER PARTY.
HE WAS 47 YEARS OLD.
CRIME SCENE D
THE END

AFTERWORD

At the time of this writing, the city of Minneapolis is on fire. It is May 27, 2020, and out of rage and frustration, protest and violence have erupted in cities throughout the United States. The cause is the death of George Floyd, a Black man killed by police officers in Minneapolis. Floyd's brutal murder was captured on video, where he can be seen lying facedown in the street, begging for his life, while an officer pushes his knee into the unarmed man's neck.

On February 23, 2020, an unarmed Black man named Ahmaud Arbery was out jogging in a suburban neighborhood in Georgia, when he was chased by three white men who killed him. The white men who killed the 25-year-old Arbery were not police officers but rather "concerned citizens" who thought the jogger might be someone involved in a string of burglaries that may or may not have happened in their neighborhood.

On March 13, 2020, in Louisville, Kentucky, a 26-year-old Black woman, Breonna Taylor, was killed while she slept. Police opened fire on Taylor's home after mistaking it for the hiding place of a felon who had already been arrested earlier that night.

It is 2020, and Minneapolis is burning because, while the year is different, the times are the same. Between 2013 and 2019, police in the United States killed 1,949 Black people. Of those nearly two thousand people, 331 were confirmed to have been unarmed. The word "confirmed" is crucial, because if history has taught us anything, it's that "it looked like he had a gun" or "I feared for my life" are considered valid justifications for the state-sanctioned killing of a Black person, be they armed or unarmed.

Writing this book broke my heart. Spending day after day researching and writing about all this death and violence took its toll. Piecing together the events that led to the deaths of Bobby Hutton, 17, and Fred Hampton, 20, left me in tears. Similarly, I know it wasn't easy for Marcus to draw this book. We talked about the significance of this work, and we checked in on each other often because, inevitably, there was always a senseless killing of a Black person in the news. These killings left us concerned about the safety of our own family and friends, and they underscored how nothing had truly changed since the 1966 killing of Denzil Dowell.

Understanding the Black Panther Party is not easy. They were a complicated group that left behind a complex legacy. It is perfectly fine if, after reading this book, you're not sure how you feel about the Panthers or you have mixed emotions. I'll admit that my personal feelings have become more nuanced over the years. Working on this project challenged much of what I knew by revealing how much I didn't know. During the process, my opinion of some members of the Party changed drastically—and not always for the better. But what any one of us thinks about the Panthers—be it positive or negative—doesn't matter nearly as much as the fact that our feelings should be derived from a place of knowledge and perhaps even some nuance.

It is impossible to know for sure what the Black Panther Party could have been had they not been targeted and undermined by the FBI's Counterintelligence Program (COINTELPRO). Instead, we are left with the complicated history of what the Black Panthers were, much of which was guided by the outside influence of law enforcement agencies determined to discredit and destroy them. To that end, it could be argued that the FBI was more successful in destroying the Panthers than the Panthers were at achieving the goals set forth in their Ten-Point Program. Aside from the constant government interference, though, the Black Panthers were not a perfect organization. Ego, pride, and personal prejudices within the party also had a hand in their undoing.

It is worth noting that, more than 50 years after Huey P. Newton and Bobby Seale founded the Black Panther Party and drafted the Ten-Point Program as their guiding manifesto, every single concern they addressed is still relevant. Every single inequity, injustice, and form of oppression impacting the Black community in 1966 is still going strong, well into the 21st century. What the Panthers wanted in 1966, we still want now. What they believed, we still know to be true.

In the end, perhaps the legacy of the Black Panthers isn't about what they may have done right versus what they may have done wrong. Perhaps it is all about the pathology of a nation so corrupted by inequality and oppression that it gave birth to the Panthers, only to then destroy what it created. Maybe it is about a system so unbalanced that armed white supremacists can march on a state capitol with no repercussions in 2020, but the Panthers were targeted as domestic terrorists for doing the same thing in 1967. Never let us forget that in the United States, Tamir Rice, a 12-year-old Black kid, was killed by police in 2014 for holding a toy gun, while the following year, Dylann Roof, a 21-year-old confirmed white supremacist, was arrested without harm after he killed nine Black people in a South Carolina church. And that is why Minneapolis is burning today.

DAVID F. WALKER
MAY 27, 2020
PORTLAND, OREGON

BIBLIOGRAPHY

Alkebulan, Paul. *Survival Pending Revolution: The History of the Black Panther Party*. Tuscaloosa: University of Alabama Press, 2007.

Austin, Curtis J. *Up Against the Wall: Violence in the Making and Unmaking of the Black Panther Party*. Fayetteville: University of Arkansas Press, 2006.

Bass, Paul, and Douglas W. Rae. *Murder in the Model City: The Black Panthers, Yale, and the Redemption of a Killer*. New York: Basic Books, 2006.

The Black Panthers: Vanguard of the Revolution. Directed by Stanley Nelson, Jr. PBS, 2015.

Bloom, Joshua, and Waldo E. Martin, Jr. *Black Against Empire: The History and Politics of the Black Panther Party*. Oakland: University of California Press, 2013.

Boyd, Herb. *Black Panthers for Beginners*. New York: Writers and Readers Publishing, Inc., 1995.

Brown, Elaine. *A Taste of Power: A Black Woman's Story*. New York: Doubleday, 1992.

Churchill, Ward, and Jim Vander Wall. *Agents of Repression: The FBI's Secret War Against the Black Panther Party and the American Indian Movement*. Boston: South End Press, 1990.

Cummins, Eric. *The Rise and Fall of California's Radical Prison Movement*. Stanford: Stanford University Press, 1994.

Davis, Angela. *Angela Davis: An Autobiography*. New York: International Publishers, 1988.

Diouf, Sylviane A., and Komozi Woodard, eds. *Black Power 50*. New York: The New Press, 2016.

Dixon, Aaron. *My People Are Rising: Memoir of a Black Panther Party Captain*. Chicago: Haymarket Books, 2012.

Douglas, Emory. *Black Panther: The Revolutionary Art of Emory Douglas*. New York: Rizzoli, 2007.

Eyes on the Prize. Produced by Henry Hampton. PBS, 1987.

Foner, Philip S., ed. *The Black Panthers Speak*. Chicago: Haymarket Books, 2014.

Forbes, Flores Alexander. *Will You Die with Me?: My Life and the Black Panther Party*. New York: Washington Square Press, 2006.

Haas, Jeffrey. *The Assassination of Fred Hampton: How the FBI and Chicago Police Murdered a Black Panther*. Chicago: Lawrence Hill Books, 2010.

Hilliard, David, ed. *The Black Panther: Intercommunal News Service 1967–1980*. New York: Atria Books, 2007.

Hilliard, David, ed. *The Black Panther Party: Service to the People Programs*. Albuquerque: University of New Mexico Press, 2008.

Hilliard, David, and Lewis Cole. *This Side of Glory: The Autobiography of David Hilliard and the Story of the Black Panther Party*. Chicago: Lawrence Hill Books, 1993.

Hilliard, David, and Donald Weise, eds. *The New Huey P. Newton Reader*. New York: Seven Stories Press, 2019.

Hilliard, David, with Keith Zimmerman and Kent Zimmerman. *Huey: Spirit of the Panther*. New York: Basic Books, 2006.

Jackson, George. *Soledad Brother: The Prison Writings of George Jackson*. Chicago: Lawrence Hill Books, 1994.

Jeffries, Hasan Kwame. *Bloody Lowndes: Civil Rights and Black Power in Alabama's Black Belt*. New York: New York University Press, 2009.

Jeffries, Judson L., ed. *Black Power in the Belly of the Beast*. Chicago: University of Illinois Press, 2006.

Jones, Charles E., ed. *The Black Panther Party [Reconsidered]*. Baltimore: Black Classic Press, 1998.

Joseph, Peniel E., ed. *The Black Power Movement: Rethinking the Civil Rights–Black Power Era*. New York: Routledge, 2006.

Lewis, Andrew B. *The Shadows of Youth: The Remarkable Journey of the Civil Rights Generation*. New York: Hill and Wang, 2009.

Look for Me in the Whirlwind: The Collective Autobiography of the New York 21. New York: Random House, 1971.

Major, Reginald. *A Panther Is a Black Cat*. Baltimore: Black Classic Press, 1971.

Marine, Gene. *The Black Panthers*. New York: Signet Books, 1969.

Morrison, Toni, ed. *To Die for the People: Huey P. Newton*. San Francisco: City Lights Books, 2009.

Nelson, Alondra. *Body and Soul: The Black Panther Party and the Fight Against Medical Discrimination*. Minneapolis: University of Minnesota Press, 2011.

Olsen, Jack. *Last Man Standing: The Tragedy and Triumph of Geronimo Pratt*. New York: Anchor Books, 2000.

Seale, Bobby. *Seize the Time: The Story of the Black Panther Party and Huey P. Newton*. Baltimore: Black Classic Press, 1970.

Shames, Stephen, and Bobby Seale. *Power to the People: The World of the Black Panthers*. New York: Abrams, 2016.

Shih, Bryan, and Yohuru Williams, eds. *The Black Panthers: Portraits from an Unfinished Revolution*. New York: Nation Books, 2016.

Spencer, Robyn C. *The Revolution Has Come: Black Power, Gender, and the Black Panther Party in Oakland*. Durham: Duke University Press, 2016.

Stewart, Sean, ed. *On the Ground: An Illustrated Anecdotal History of the Sixties Underground Press in the U.S.* Oakland: PM Press, 2011.

Swearingen, M. Wesley. *FBI Secrets: An Agent's Exposé*. Boston: South End Press, 1995.

Van Peebles, Mario, Ula Y. Taylor, and J. Tarika Lewis. *Panther: A Pictorial History of the Black Panthers and the Story Behind the Film*. New York: Newmarket Press, 1995.

Wilkins, Roy, and Ramsey Clark. *Search and Destroy: A Report by the Commission of Inquiry into the Black Panthers and the Police*. New York: Metropolitan Applied Research Center, 1973.

ACKNOWLEDGMENTS

DAVID F. WALKER: I would like to thank everyone who helped make this book possible, starting with Marcus, an incredible artist and collaborator. Much appreciation to Billy X. Jennings, who has tirelessly worked to document and archive the history of the Black Panther Party (and thanks to Aaron Grizzell for the introduction). My undying respect and gratitude to all the historians and academics who have faced the challenges of recounting the history of the BPP (it is not easy). Thanks to everyone at Ten Speed Press for their support of this book and for their commitment to the medium of graphic novels. Thanks to the Glass Literary Agency and Alex Glass for looking out for me. Undying gratitude to the Multnomah County Library, University of California's Calisphere archive, and Bay Area Television Archive for all the research material. Thanks to Team Bitter Root (Chuck and Sanford). Thanks to my best friend and business partner, Sean Owolo. And, finally, an extra special thanks to my mother, Bonnie Walker.

MARCUS KWAME ANDERSON: I'd like to thank my wife and daughter for their love, support, and inspiration. Thanks to David for his talent, vision, and the incredible amount of work and care that he put into this book. Many thanks to everyone at Ten Speed Press for providing me with the opportunity to be a part of telling this important story. Thank you to Alexandria Batchelor for the assistance. Much love to those who have stood up to injustice and fought to create a better world. Respect to the youth carrying the torch. Thank you to Mrs. Pace and all of the teachers who encouraged this lanky kid with a sketchbook to keep drawing. Thanks to my mother, father, and brother for being my foundation. Much love to the crew for decades of laughter and real talk. Thanks to Leo and my BCC team. Eternal thanks to the entire village of family, friends, elders, mentors, and collaborators who have walked with me.

ABOUT AUTHOR

DAVID F. WALKER is an award-winning comic book writer, filmmaker, journalist, and educator. His writing career started in the 1990s with the self-published zine *BadAzz MoFo*. In 1997, he produced and directed *Macked, Hammered, Slaughtered, and Shafted*, a feature-length documentary on the history of blaxploitation films. Walker is best known for his work in graphic novels and comics, which includes *The Life of Frederick Douglass* (Ten Speed Press), the Eisner Award–winning series *Bitter Root* (Image Comics), and the critically acclaimed series *Naomi* (DC Comics). He has written for Marvel Comics (*Luke Cage, Occupy Avengers, Power Man and Iron Fist, Nighthawk, Fury, Deadpool*), DC Comics (*Cyborg, Young Justice*), Dynamite Entertainment (*Shaft*), and Dark Horse (*Number 13*). He teaches part time at Portland State University.

ABOUT THE ILLUSTRATOR

MARCUS KWAME ANDERSON is an illustrator, fine artist, and teacher. Much of his work explores the beauty and diversity of the African diaspora. He graduated from SUNY Fredonia with a degree in illustration. Anderson is the co-creator of the comic book series *Snow Daze* and has illustrated stories in Action Lab's series *Cash and Carrie* and *F.O.R.C.E.* He has many stories left to tell.

INDEX

Ten Speed Press and the Ten Speed Press colophon are registered
trademarks of Penguin Random House LLC.

Library of Congress Cataloging-in-Publication Data
Names: Walker, David, 1968- author. | Anderson, Marcus Kwame, 1976- illustrator.
Title: Black Panther Party / David F. Walker ; art and colors by Marcus Kwame Anderson.
Description: First edition. | Emeryville, California : Ten Speed Press,
    [2021] | Includes bibliographical references and index.
Identifiers: LCCN 2020004441 (print) | LCCN 2020004442 (ebook) |
    ISBN 9781984857705 (trade paperback) | ISBN 9781984857712 (ebook)
Subjects: LCSH: Black Panther Party—Comic books, strips, etc. | Black power—
    United States—Comic books, strips, etc. | African Americans—Politics and
    government—Comic books, strips, etc. | Graphic novels.
Classification: LCC E185.615 .W275 2021 (print) | LCC E185.615 (ebook) |
    DDC 322.4/20973—dc23
LC record available at https://lccn.loc.gov/2020004441
LC ebook record available at https://lccn.loc.gov/2020004442

Trade Paperback ISBN: 978-1-9848-5770-5
eBook ISBN: 978-1-9849-5771-2

Printed in Italy

Editor: Kaitlin Ketchum
Designer: Chloe Rawlins
Colorist and Letterer: Marcus Kwame Anderson | Assistant Colorist: Alexandria Batchelor
Production manager: Serena Sigona
Copyeditor: Amelia Iuvino | Proofreader: Kate Bolen | Indexer: Ken Della Penta
Publicist: Natalie Yera | Marketer: Daniel Wikey

10 9 8 7 6 5 4 3 2 1

First Edition